I ONLY HAVE TROUBLE WITH PEOPLE...

Lynn Bilek Edmonds

I
  ONLY
    HAVE
      TROUBLE
        WITH
          PEOPLE…

Copyright @ 2006 Lynn Bilek Edmonds
All rights reserved.
ISBN: 0-615-18477-4

www.IOnlyHaveTroubleWithPeople.com
(Link to www.Amazon.com)

For my husband Joey, whose constant badgering made this book possible.
I love you dear.

Special Thanks:

To my son and daughter, Grant and Kate.
To my brother Dale Bilek.
To his wife, Judith Drake Bilek.
…truly my family of editors.

To Dan Schneider for your creative cover.

MUSINGS

I ONLY HAVE TROUBLE WITH PEOPLE…

...who don't do what they say they are going to do------------------ 1
...who look at their passengers when driving-------------------------2
...who marry because they need the other person--------------------4
...who think football is less creative than the ARTS-----6
...who use cell phones---7
...who blame teachers---8
...who don't like animals-- 9
...who are not loyal…to their TV series---------------------10
...who have forgotten how to dream-------------------------------------12
...who can't say "I don't know"-------------------------------------- 13
...who don't like to move---14
...who are unhappy mothers---------------------------------16
...who cannot make a decision--- 18
...who read bedtimes stories to small children----------------------19
...who complain about their looks------------------------------------20
...who can't see beyond themselves--------------------22
...who don't speak correct English-------------------------------23
...who have separation issues--24
...who think rap is music--26
...who relish reunions-------------------------------------28
...who overdo it with the salt--29
...who don't understand the traditions of baseball----------- 30
...who send greeting cards by e-mail-----------------------------32
...who can not see any difference between the two
       political parties --------------------------------- 33
...who get up early in the morning when they
       don't have to--34
...who encourage 'Little Bunny Foo Foo'----------------------- 36
...who think there must be silence ---------------------------------37
...who are TV Programmers------------------------- 38
...who go crazy with the paperwork--------------------------------39
...who don't pray---41

I ONLY HAVE TROUBLE WITH PEOPLE…

...who don't read newspapers---42
...who can't sit still-- 43
...who support girls only/boys only soccer ----------------------------44
...who keep up with their reading---------------------------47
...who won't eat anything fattening-------------------------------------49
...who make Saturday Night Live sketches into movies-------------51
...who use digital cameras--52
...who scroll-- 53
...who are silent fathers---55
...who frown on the word "liberal"------------------------------------- 57
...who think higher is better-- 58
...who don't frequent live theatre--------------------------- 59
...who don't worry about things--- 61
...who have no wedding manners---------------------------------------62
...who don't prioritize---63
...who talk when you're talking to someone else
         on the telephone---65
...who take babies on long airplane trips------------------------------ 66
...who blame God--- 67
...who don't know how to cheer--- 68
...who misuse data---70
...who swear around young and old people----------------------------71
...who don't smile when their picture is being taken------------------72
...who debunk astrology---73
...who misuse the word "elite"---------------------------------75
...who don't teach their children how to behave pool side----------76
...who do not think being cheap is a virtue----------------------------77
...who are against gun regulations-------------------------------------78
...who tease children--79
...who must always do something---------------------------------------81
...who buy into stereotypes---82
...who don't have a passion-- 83
...who don't care how they appear to others------------ 84
...who don't like to play games--86
...who crowd the airport baggage carousel------------------------- 88

I ONLY HAVE TROUBLE WITH PEOPLE…

…who constantly win at the race track----------------------------- 89
…who are pseudo scientists-------------------------------- 90
…who wave things at basketball games----------------------------- 91
…who have no weaknesses-- 92
…who won't compromise---93
…who teach their children to be loud--------------------94
…who like high heels-- 95
…who still smoke--- 96
…who threaten children-- 98
…who try too hard to make people laugh--------------100
…who only believe what they want to believe---------------------- 101
…who grow up too fast--102
…who are security risks---104
…who are chauvinists--105
…who do not understand boobs-------------------------------------- 107
…who distance themselves from the ocean---------------------------109
…who don't vote-- 111
…who do vote--113
…who don't like to cook-- 114
…who can't admit they have lied--116
…who just drop by-- 117
…who don't give credit when credit is due------------118
…who can grow things--- 119
…who bring stuff---121
…who have not vacationed at a dude ranch----------------------- 122
…who don't respect their limitations--------------------124
…who make you wonder why you want to eat out------------------125
…who try to make everything equal----------------------------------127
…who never had long hair---129
…who do not pick up after themselves---------------- 130
…who shower every single day of their lives------------------------131
…who take up too much space---------------------------------------132
…who tell me things I just don't want to know----------------------133
…who never change their mind-------------------------134
…who don't have trouble with people----------------------------------135
…who can't step back---136

I ONLY HAVE TROUBLE WITH PEOPLE…

…who don't do what they say they are going to do. So here I am writing this book. About a year ago, I came up with the thought " I only have trouble with people." Everyone I mentioned it to…that would be my husband…said "What a terrific title for a book!" I made the point, or thought I had, that this would be kept secret, perhaps a private enterprise for my own amusement… a personal mind game. This was before I found out that my husband had let it slip…blurted out, in fact, MY TITLE to several relatives, friends, acquaintances, etc. I found myself in social situations being asked the usual,
"What is it that you do?"

"Well, I used to be an actress, before I had my kids, blah, blah, blah."

"Your kids are adults. What is it that you do now?"

"Well, there's this book I'm thinking…"

"Oh, you're a writer!"

So there I was, facing a conundrum. If I only have trouble with people who don't do what they say they are going to do and I was not writing a book, I was having trouble with myself. That could not stand.

I ONLY HAVE TROUBLE WITH PEOPLE...

who look at their passengers when driving. Now, I don't even drive. Never have. Unless you count bumper cars and golf carts. (I'm not even good at that!) But I have observed drivers whose heads are definitely turned to the right while chatting away on the highway. I instinctively feel that when the driver's eyes are not on the road, the traveling experience becomes more dangerous.

When conversing with another in an automobile, there is hardly any need to make eye contact. You know who you're talking to. You know who's in your car. It's not as if you can't keep up your end of the conversation unless you see the person you're addressing. Most of us are not in the habit of using picture phones. If the conversation is so heated, that you feel absolutely compelled to look at the person, this is definitely the wrong place and the wrong time. As would be, being so in love that you can't bear to take your eyes off of him or her.

I can only assume that the driver has, for the moment, forgotten he was in charge of 1000 pounds of steel …in motion…at high speed. This type of driver assumes this responsibility with way too great a deal of nonchalance. They should remember they're not on a horse. Granted, a horse could present different problems, but at least, a horse could swerve away from a tree it may be steered toward. A horse could react in such a way it would not run into a person or another horse. One should be able to remember a car does not have a brain. And until someone invents an automobile that drives itself, the chatterbox driver should keep eyes on the road …and I promise never to drive.

I ONLY HAVE TROUBLE WITH PEOPLE...

...who marry because they need the other person. If you literally believe you need someone else to make you whole or to complete your life, you are admitting to gross inadequacy. No one is without faults. But if you are saying, "I am so insufficient I need an entire other person to give me justification for being," who in their right mind would want to marry you? That I think is the key. I think two people should marry because they WANT TO, not need to. Why should anyone want to complicate their life? One person should complement the life of the other. The difference between those words, complicate and complement could be the difference between a successful or an unsuccessful marriage. Concentrate on what you, your unique self, can bring to the relationship, the qualities you and you alone can share with the one you love. No one should expect perfection. Setting the bar too high could bring about unnecessary problems and pressure.
(See Musing… I only have trouble with people who think higher is better)

If needs go unmet, most likely the needy person is going to blame the other for not satisfying them. But if you have a fairly good and honest understanding of yourself and if you can communicate this to your partner and visa versa, you need not depend on the other to fulfill your needs. You need not suffer major disappointment in your relationship.

To paraphrase JFK, "Ask not what your partner can do for you—ask what you can do for your partner."

I ONLY HAVE TROUBLE WITH PEOPLE…

…who think football is less creative than the ARTS. Granted, Walter Payton was no Salvador Dali or Picasso. Joe Namath was no Tennessee Williams or Eugene O'Neill. Artists starting out with a blank slate don't have to follow a game plan. They do not have anybody else calling the plays. But Johnny Depp does. As one of the finest actors of his generation, his art is most often determined by scripted lines and confined to hitting his spot. Plus, he has an entire creative team working together toward a common goal.

In football, the player is facing opposing players who are not on the same page. In fact, the other team is violently trying to disrupt your game plan. That would demand the individual players be very creative, if only to avoid unnecessary bodily harm.

Singers and musicians are well defined by their art form. More freedom in the arts is available to comedians, but even the most inventive improv artists have some idea of where they are going. They like their laughs, but if they're not forthcoming, rest assured they have surefire material to fall back on. What can a footballer fall back on? He can't even rely on the ball.

I ONLY HAVE TROUBLE WITH PEOPLE…

…who use cell phones. I'm old enough to remember when only the top celebrities, seated in customized booths at the best restaurants in the world…the Pump Room in the Ambassador East, Chicago…the Derby in Hollywood…had access to private telephones when out in public. Quite a symbol of being in the top echelon of society … an unmistakable sign of POPULARITY! Isn't it amazing how nowadays so many of us are members of the "in" crowd? And if others seem not to notice, how LOUD we can be about it?

I happen to think that anything that is so commonplace is not necessarily worth having. The lowest common denominator should not be considered a status symbol. The fact that one is on call at all times to all callers is demeaning. Where is your self-esteem? Is this not a sign of inferiority? Do you really need virtually constant reaffirmation of your existence? I will allow for some necessary business calls and certainly the benefits of safety or emergency use.
But really!

I ONLY HAVE TROUBLE WITH PEOPLE…

…who blame teachers. It is not uncommon that students complain, " School is boring." When questioned further, the charge generally becomes more specific, because their friends are cool, their extra curricular activities are fun and, oh yeah, most of their classes are interesting. It's just his one "prof" who is BORING. Generally, teachers have some knowledge to impart. At least, they have more information than the student. There would be something that the student could gain from paying attention. Therefore, it is the student's responsibility, it is the job of the "teachee" to challenge him/herself to find something in the subject that is interesting, i.e. not boring. Teachers are not entertainers. It helps if they have attractive personalities and if their fascination with their subject transfers to their students. I would argue that a student would be hard pressed not to have chanced upon some such teachers during their school years. That's just the luck of the draw. So, when dealt a lowly pair of deuces, declare them wild.

I ONLY HAVE TROUBLE WITH PEOPLE...

...who don't like animals. I'm not saying that everyone should have a pet...although those in animal shelters would certainly benefit. And I am not advocating that zoos and circuses should "let their creatures go." Nor do I think there is cruelty in horseracing, rodeos or dog shows. I just think there is a connection to be made. People who lack an appreciation for our furry, feathered, hairy or scaly friends are missing out on one of the greatest pleasures in life. Whether you have a wonderful personal relationship as a pet owner or you enjoy their beauty or magnificence from a distance, there is an added dimension to be experienced. Don't miss out.

ONLY HAVE TROUBLE WITH PEOPLE...

...who are not loyal ...to their TV series. I think most of us like to connect with friends or family. One of many ways to do so is to watch the same shows. Although you probably are unable to physically do so, you still can enjoy later discussions about them, even retelling jokes to share a laugh or revisiting moments challenging each other's memory. It can be kind of a game.

I find it nearly impossible to keep up with all the new shows, so it's only natural to take the advice of others. It seems logical that your friend's taste would be similar to your own. It would be worth your while to take a look at what they like. I'll generally give the program a couple of viewings. After that, I'll be honest and admit whether I'm going to keep with it. The problem arises when I get hooked on a series only to discover the person who encouraged me to watch it is no longer a fan. The captain has abandoned the ship.

Is this a question of loyalty to the series or is this a symptom of a deeper problem...loyalty to you? Does this signify a fault in your relationship? Your friend is fickle? Your friend doesn't know what he/she likes?

Will your friend drop you just as easily as that television show? And not tell you about it? What should you do? Should you stop watching because you no longer have someone to share it with? You're still enjoying it. Does that mean your friend has better taste than you do? Is there inherent snobbery here? Aw, come off it. We're talkin' television.

ONLY HAVE TROUBLE WITH PEOPLE...

...who have forgotten how to dream.
Practically as soon as children can talk they are answering the question, "What do you want to be when you grow up?" The answers can be simple. " I want to be just like my daddy/mommy." Realistic: "a teacher"… a "doctor/nurse." More risky: "a fireman"… "a policeman." Idealistic: "an astronaut"… "the president." More fanciful: "a movie star." Practically impossible: " a millionaire"…" a basketball player." Yet only the coldest hearted adult would reply, "Don't be silly. You can't do that." So these children continue on and become teenagers who daydream. They may not tell us that they are daydreaming or what they're daydreaming about, but you can bet it's a preferred pastime.

   I don't profess to know when most people stop dreaming. It probably happens to people at different times of their lives, when the real world starts to intrude on privacy. But, consider this. Maybe the dreams have just been put on the back burner for a while. They can always be rekindled. And, of course, they don't have to be the same dreams. I mean, I wanted to be a cowboy before I realized that would be a cowgirl. Now, at my age, I hardly consider that dream at all. But there are others. And they're fun.

ONLY HAVE TROUBLE WITH PEOPLE…

…who can't say "I don't know." Why is it that some people can't seem to admit they don't know everything? Surely, there are what ?… billions or trillions of subjects in this wide world of ours and the details and intricacies of those subjects must be unfathomable. So, why should someone be ashamed to say they don't understand something? Think of all the time that could be saved if, when a topic is mentioned, those who know nothing about it just kept quiet. This could facilitate an interesting discussion, where a serious exchange of ideas and perhaps knowledge could possibly occur. I also find when I tell someone " I don't know about such and such," that can act as my exit line. I have previously mentioned that I don't drive a car, so it seems logical that I do not follow NASCAR. So when such a subject enters the conversation, which seems to be happening more and more as of late, I plead ignorance and you know what? People are generally glad to see me excuse myself. Just because I don't know something doesn't necessarily mean I want to. I may simply not care and I don't wish to bring down those who do. Does that seem fair?
  " I don't know."

I ONLY HAVE TROUBLE WITH PEOPLE…

…who don't like to move. Sure there's packing to be done. Sure there's all sorts of arrangements to be made…all sorts of people to notify. You just need to welcome the chaos.

You can't ignore the excitement of chaos. This is a time filled with opportunity. Look at it as a chance at a new beginning. New beginnings don't come around that often, as is clearly seen by the amount of junk you've probably accumulated in the current space you occupy. Now would be the time to throw things out by the truckload. What a relief! You get to decide what is important enough to you to be given a place in the wagon train. You can also donate items to charity or thrift shops en mass. If you have experienced the feeling of satisfaction in giving before, your self-congratulations could reach an all time high. As a general rule, you would pack kitchen items with kitchen items, books with books, clothes with clothes, etc. This is a chance to be the most organized you've ever been in your whole life. And the cleanest! Only the very worst of us would pack dirty dishes. Who would want to bring along their old germs?   EWW!

Fast forward to the actual arrival of the movers. How often do you get to order around several large, hulky men for a few hours? "The couch goes over there. Take the dining room table to the dining room. Those boxes belong in the basement." Such a feeling of power. Makes no difference whether you're male or female. It's a power rush.

Of course, everything can be taken to the extreme. I have a husband who just really, really likes to move things. Leave him alone in the dining room and the dining room table will be facing in a different direction than when last you ate. If you should hear loud banging and groaning coming from the second floor, that could only mean that beds and couches and desks and dressers are switching locations. I guess it's a harmless activity. Except for his back.

I ONLY HAVE TROUBLE WITH PEOPLE...

...who are unhappy mothers. I was an actress. That training was for me, and I would propose could be for others, a great aid in mothering. One technique is "being in the moment." I would say from babyhood throughout elementary school that's where your child is. It would behoove you to be there too. This method requires focusing your attention on the action at hand. It might also mean multitasking. When in a supermarket with a toddler, a shopping list and a bustling array of people and products, this can be challenging. A good place to start might be not wishing you were anywhere else, but where you are. Preparation for the outing, in acting terms "a rehearsal," could help to set the stage for a decent performance. Most kids love to "act out." "Play" is the name of their game.

Day-by day, interacting with children seems to alternate between ordinary activities heightened to the dramatic and ordinary activities of monotonous routine. When dealing with those necessary rituals, whether it's brushing teeth or reading the same story for the umpteenth time, "actors" can revert to "the illusion of the first time."

This concept, basically a version of "Let's Pretend" allows actors to perform, successfully, the same role night after night in a lengthy theatrical run. Frankly, practically my whole philosophy of parenting was based on these few acting principles.

  My now young adult children have told me that they think I should have paid them for all the enjoyment I had raising them. When my son was discussing his past with a psychologist, the psychologist thought perhaps he had had a too trouble-free childhood. Personally, I don't think there could be such a thing. But even if there is, isn't that preferable to the all too prevalent troubled childhood? An all too frequent harried mother and frazzled child? I turned down the role of the harried mother.

I ONLY HAVE TROUBLE WITH PEOPLE...

...who cannot make a decision. Some people have grave difficulties in ordering from a restaurant menu. Just too many choices. But that's the whole point of dining out. You are not being made to eat whatever your mother puts on the table. You are not the unwitting victim of an ever experimenting hostess. You get to make a choice. Surely, you can eliminate some of the items, simply because you don't like them. You probably can eliminate others because of prices you don't like. If you make a mistake, you can chalk it up to an epicurean learning experience. Anyway, this is not a matter of life or death. In fact, over a lifetime very few decisions that the average person has to make are. That is comforting in and of itself.

What is not comforting are the decisions and indecisions of people in government which affect our private lives. I don't know, but it appears to me, that intrusive judgments by the government are lessening our ability to make our own decisions. That could be called brainwashing. Anyone who is brainwashed is incapable of making decisions. I don't want Big Brother ordering my soup.

I ONLY HAVE TROUBLE WITH PEOPLE…

…who read bedtime stories to small children. I know that this is for some a time-honored tradition. What could be more tender than lovingly tucking the child into bed, softly reading or rereading a classic tale until the wee one drifts off into peaceful slumber? Well, I don't believe that teaching a child, maybe subconsciously, that books put you to sleep or should put you to sleep is a good lesson for them to learn.

    I am all for reading to and with your child, but it should be an activity. It should be an interactive, exciting, enjoyable time. Anytime during the day or early evening, the two, three or more of you can share a rather calm, relatively quiet and hopefully thoughtful literary experience. Wow! That's special. That's what I call "quality time."

I ONLY HAVE TROUBLE WITH PEOPLE...

...who complain about their looks. I was born lopsided. Every time I look in the mirror I see a pair of eyes that are not level and two sides of a face that are not symmetrical. I was born with a condition they told me was called rye neck...a cord within the right side of my neck was tighter and stronger than the opposing one on the left. That threw the whole facial thing out of whack and caused my scoliosis, which is probably going to cause major future problems.

As a kid, these differences seemed monumental. The scoliosis could basically remain hidden, but nobody can avoid seeing a face. Somehow as I went about my business of being me, I became what kids call popular and I discovered that kids don't make fun of kids who are popular. I don't recall anybody ever saying, "Hey, do you know your face is weird?" Was I just fortunate to have an unusually kind, thoughtful, empathetic group of peers? In a rather diverse, inner-city school of Chicago? I think not.

What's more, I went outside of this protective environment and auditioned for plays, as well as modeling jobs. Now I know in a theatre, no one, even in the very first row, is going to notice the dissimilarities of your face. Nor would they on a runway. But in a print ad? I made it into the pages of Seventeen!

Much, much later on in my life, I did meet someone who said something to me, right to my face, about my face. He said, "It's like looking in the mirror." I married him.

I ONLY HAVE TROUBLE WITH PEOPLE…

…who can't see beyond themselves. You know what really bothers me in the supermarket checkout line? No, it's not the person who brought more than 10 items to the 10 items or less line. I've come to the conclusion that some people just can't count. No, it's the person who waits until her bill has been calculated to search for her checkbook or wallet in her cavernous purse. It's as if she is taken by surprise that payment would be called for. The search is never easy. And I don't mean to suggest that this is merely a feminine problem. Granted, a guy usually can find his wallet rather quickly…in his back pocket, in his jacket pocket. I mean, there can only be so many pockets. But where that credit or debit card could be inside that wallet? Oh, that's the bedevilment! Don't these people realize there are other patrons in the store, other people waiting in line? This might be the highlight of the day for these clueless folk, but it's really not the time or the place to make oneself the center of attention.

I ONLY HAVE TROUBLE WITH PEOPLE…

…who don't speak correct English. Now I'm not talking about persons who have English as their second language. In fact, I admire them greatly for attempting to communicate in something other than their native tongue. I know I tried my darndest in college to learn French. I struggled for two years, after which I could honestly answer the question,
 "Parlez vous Francais?"
 "Un peu."
 The people I'm concerned about were raised in the United States. They somehow managed their way through the years of required education without getting a feel or developing an ear for the customary use of English. I know there is the ever perplexing "lie or lay." But the proper use of pronouns is simply a matter of whether the pronoun is the subject or the object of a sentence or a preposition. "Bob and her are going to a movie." No they're not. "Do Bob's parents approve of Bob and she dating"? Uh. Uh. Sometimes it may take a moment to think of the correct wording. But when did it become prudent not to think before speaking?

I ONLY HAVE TROUBLE WITH PEOPLE…

…who have separation issues. I would assume we have all seen or been participants ourselves in the emotional experience of that first day of school. It is often the first time child and parent are parted for any length of time. The child often is eager for the new experience. It is the parent who finds the separation almost unbearable.

How can this be? Does the parent feel she/he has not prepared their child adequately to face the unknown? Does the parent feel her/his parenting skills will be put to the test and be found lacking? Is the parent so immature that she/he is emotionally dependent on the child? This is role reversal in the worst possible scenario. The nervousness, the anxiety and the insecurity transfer to the child. What a burden to put on a little person! They begin to doubt themselves and the wisdom of this situation. "What is this thing called SCHOOL? It's terrorizing my mother!"

Add to this the guilt the child must feel for putting his loving parent in such a state! Way to begin on a promising path of education.

Fast forward some twelve years. These are the same folks who will suffer from "the empty nest syndrome" when their child enters college. I'm sorry. I can't sympathize. This is a great opportunity to be a cheerleader. What an exciting time lies ahead for the young adult who is fortunate enough to attend college. Don't be a spoil sport. Help choose that new wardrobe. Even help decorate the dorm room. Then go home and turn that empty bedroom into a guest room or a mausoleum. Your pick!
I think it's time for the grown-ups to grow up.

I ONLY HAVE TROUBLE WITH PEOPLE…

…who think rap is music. Honestly, I'm not a fan. I have never consciously sat down and given my full, undivided attention for any length of time to try to get with it and understand it. I'm not hip, not alone hip-hop. (Poor joke) But there is no way to completely avoid hearing it. I can't comprehend most of the words, which is probably just as well, because I gather there is much that is inflammatory. I'm a big "DEADWOOD" fan though, so if profanity is used as an artful device, I can be won over.

If the language is clear, maybe rap should be considered poetry. I still can't find my way to classify it as music. The Funk & Wagnalls Standard Desk Dictionary defines music as "the art of producing significant arrangements of sounds, usu. with reference to rhythm, pitch, and tone color." Granted, rap has rhythm, but so does poetry. Variety of pitch seems so negligible, how can there be significant arrangement? Likewise tone color.

I feel the real reason that rap shouldn't be considered music lies in the future. One of the pure pleasures of growing old is reminiscing about the songs of your youth. My parents had "You Are My Sunshine." My generation has "Rudolph, the Red-Nosed Reindeer." But people have memory problems when they age. Sometimes you just can't remember the words. Rappers do not have a prayer!

I ONLY HAVE TROUBLE WITH PEOPLE...

...who relish reunions. There seem to be those who love to attend these gatherings. No sooner is the evening over than they are planning for the next one. It's not good enough to hold a 10 year, 25 year or 50 year reunion. Their class should get together every 5 years or as the years go by, every 4 years maybe.

 I think the spouse of the invitee should be given more consideration. Perhaps the couple who fell in love during their school days would equally enjoy reliving the past and catching up on the present with their old classmates. But I dare say, those couples are few and far between, if indeed they are still together. The spouse who didn't share all those experiences can't honestly be that interested. He/she didn't fall in love with a teenager. The spouse met and married an individual farther along in life and hopefully more mature. Your mate in high school would be a stranger to you. You are placed in a situation from another dimension, another world, another time. You are hearing things you can never truly understand. You were not there. How can others' reminiscences make for a comfortable evening? Anyway, I assume many just smile, while gritting their teeth, and try to be as cordial as possible. And say to their partner afterward, "You owe me one."

I ONLY HAVE TROUBLE WITH PEOPLE…

…who overdo it with the salt. I guess I just like food too much, and I think I'm a halfway decent cook, which may allow me to take this point of view. Too often I see people, who as soon as the waiter sets down their plate, reach for the saltshaker and pour. They haven't even taken a bite, given it a little taste test. Certainly, every dish a waiter has ever placed before them hasn't had the same degree of seasoning. Of course, how would they know? They have never eaten anything that wasn't loaded with salt. Many would suggest that this practice is detrimental to your good health. That's an excellent reason to reconsider this habit. Another may be simply, don't miss out on one of the joys of living, the appreciation of good food. Your taste buds are not being given a fair chance, provided they have not been completely destroyed all ready. If I were a restaurant owner, I wouldn't put saltshakers on the tables. But from what I've witnessed, I probably wouldn't be in business very long.
 P.S. Ketchup lovers, reread this paragraph and substitute the word ketchup for salt.

I ONLY HAVE TROUBLE WITH PEOPLE...

...who don't understand the traditions of baseball. I am talking about fans, people who go to the games, who know the game, who root for and follow their team. To these fans, I'm talking about the seventh inning stretch. I probably have to blame this on Harry Carey, the legendary sports announcer who popularized the singing of "Take Me Out To The Ballgame." Halfway through the seventh inning, the crowd, led by Harry, would rise and belt out this hymn. That's fine if you're the home team. You sing or yell, whatever, before your team comes to bat. But...if you are a fan of the opposition and you have made that extra fanatic effort to travel into enemy territory to support your team, you need to stand and stretch at the top of the inning before the visiting team comes to bat.

In the "olden" days, generally the majority would take their seventh inning stretch before the bottom of the seventh and those brave outsiders, at the top. There wasn't any singing then. Just standing and stretching. But since Harry, "Take Me Out To The Ballgame" is almost a mandatory part of the baseball experience at ballparks throughout the nation.

The difficulty is that the visiting team's fans find it impossible not to join in, especially since the huge scoreboards are flashing the words in your face and the stadium is rockin'. It's simply irresistible. But in doing so, you are rooting for the wrong side.

   So, my advice to you is do what I do… a lifelong Cubbie fan, who so far has followed the Cubs from Wrigley Field to San Diego, via Shea Stadium and Los Angeles. Stand up at the top of the seventh. When your half of the inning is over, keep seated. Do sing, but don't stretch. That's the plan.

I ONLY HAVE TROUBLE WITH PEOPLE…

…who send greeting cards by e-mail. I have received some terrific birthday cards that are wonderfully creative, particularly the ones that sing and dance. Love 'em. So inventive and, well, just "in." But, I'm a "saver." Sometimes I keep my favorite paper cards for years and years and probably will forever. I may not look back at them very often, but when I do, I get to enjoy those memories all over again. I can't do that with the e-mail ones. They're gone and I'm afraid pretty easily forgotten. And I don't think that's just because of any short-term memory loss. Seems a shame.

I know it must be a real convenience for the sender. They didn't have to actually make a trip to a card store and spend an appreciable amount of time searching through the aisles to select that "perfect" card. What's more, they didn't have to remember a week in advance that a "special date" was approaching. There's no need to panic. No last minute dashing about. No embarrassed shopping in the belated card section. No one will know you forgot. Just zip that e-mail card out today on the very day in question. Oh no, you don't. I think you should be held accountable. I want a paper trail.

I ONLY HAVE TROUBLE WITH PEOPLE...

...who can not see any difference between the two major political parties. Pundits may declare that only one party is pro-choice, pro-gun control and pro-same sex marriage. Yet there are party affiliates, voters of both parties, who take those stands. So, I guess to a certain extent, one could say there is no clear distinction between the two on these issues. Maybe only a matter of degrees. And if just a matter of degrees, there could be possible common ground upon which to build a consensus.

Compromise? Never! The 75% and the 25% shall never meet. That is not the argument the advocates, who detect no dissimilarity, wish to accept. They want to emphasize the close ties between government and big business. In fact, the ownership of both parties by corporations. The indebtedness, the basis for "quid pro quo", of corrupt government.

Once again, I believe, it's a matter of degrees. If one party sides with Big Business almost 100% of the time, negating issues important to the Little Guy, such as safety, health and security, and the other party weighs the consequences of such decisions, probably the degree of "quid pro quo" would be quite a bit less. Degrees do matter. Ask Kevin Bacon.

I ONLY HAVE TROUBLE WITH PEOPLE…

…who get up early in the morning when they don't have to. I have never been the type who jumps out of bed eager to meet the new day. Yet, if it is necessary for me to set an alarm clock, I usually don't automatically hit the snooze button. I generally remember the reason I had to summon my body at a certain hour and arise accordingly, if not enthusiastically. It's not the worst thing in the world. But when my hour to awaken is set by my own personal time clock, it's not even a temptation to actually physically get out of bed upon the dawn of first consciousness. I go slow. Unless of course, it's a potty call, which nowadays can happen anytime during the night or early wee hours of the morning. Then I gently retreat to the bathroom, carefully trying not to wake up my entire body. If you can successfully complete the task in somewhat of a stupor, falling quickly back to sleep is a snap. I shouldn't put it that way. A snap is too loud. However, if awakening for the day is the eventual plan, I do go slowly.

The pleasure of rolling over is not to be underestimated. How many other chances during the day do you get the chance to roll over? And in such comfort?
　Probably when going to bed at night, you don't really notice how fluffy that pillow feels or how comfy the mattress may be or how soft the sheets are or how warm the blankie is. This is your chance to arouse the senses. This is the time to stretch. Physically, it's not as hard when horizontal. Mentally, this can be a time to think, make a plan, set a mental picture for the day, (maybe pray). Sometimes I try to remember my dreams. Weird? Don't think so, just hard to do. Then again, you can always simply go back to sleep.

I ONLY HAVE TROUBLE WITH PEOPLE...

...who encourage "Little Bunny Foo Foo." For those who are not aware of the children's song, "Little Bunny Foo Foo" is a catchy tune that can be likened to a musical version of Whack-a-Mole. The lead character goes happily hopping through the forest, finding field mice and bopping them on the head...over and over and over again. The ending of the piece is a cute pun, but much too nuanced for the kindergarten set. The message introduced, emphasized and received is the pure joy of bopping things on the head. And of course, the children are encouraged to gesture wildly as they sing along. Now, I think, it is not in anyone's best interest to promote this world view at such an early age. If anything, one should want to steer the young into the opposite direction. It's not uncommon to hear adults say, when dealing with this age group, the simple words, " No hitting." "We do not hit." Of course, I'm assuming the adult is following his/her own advice on this matter. Besides, what's wrong with "Itsy Bitsy Spider?"

I ONLY HAVE TROUBLE WITH PEOPLE...

...who think there must be silence. Who came up with the bright idea that in order to fully concentrate there must be complete quiet? Certainly in a classroom situation, a teacher needs a fair amount of order to focus the students' attention, but the teacher does not have control of the students' concentration. Why is it necessary that a kid in his room doing homework has to turn off the radio or the music? I'm not advocating watching television at that time, because eyes AND ears would be involved. That would be way too much of a challenge. However, I do find that audio rhythms can be a driving force. The very act of blocking out the sound concentrates ones' attention on the subject matter, whereas silence tempts the mind to wander. There's a need to fill up the vacuum and not necessarily with the task at hand. What's more, when the student's attention needs to take a break, the background noise keeps the momentum going. It would be easier for the student to get back into the groove and complete the work. That's my theory. How else could I keep writing this book? Don't touch that dial!

I ONLY HAVE TROUBLE WITH PEOPLE…

…who are TV programmers. I am writing this while waiting for the return of the repairman with our television set. Without the aid of TiVo, it is nearly impossible to know in advance what will be on the screen this day and night. You may consult your daily newspaper, but those listings are different than the ones in, say, the TV Guide. Even when wishing to TiVo 'first run only', if there is no release of information concerning the program, if guests or titles are not provided, your television will be overloaded with shows you do not wish to see. Then, there are the various interpretations of the "season." New shows now premiere in the fall, as well as, in the summer. There are also mid-season replacements. A series can be 6 episodes, or 13 or 22. Series may be canceled before all their episodes are aired. This is particularly disturbing with an unsolved mystery! Even with returning shows, the new season, whenever that is, does not guarantee that a program will be on the same day at the same time, where it was successful, when it returns. Doesn't that put a successful show in unnecessary jeopardy? In the beginning, you could watch either wrestling or screen patterns. Then along came TV programmers.

I ONLY HAVE TROUBLE WITH PEOPLE…

…who go crazy with the paperwork. I think there are people who believe that just because we have access to lots of different office machinery we should use them all. I don't know how many times our office has received faxes, only to receive by mail the very same papers a day or two later. I think that whoever sent them had an irrepressible urge to use that fax machine, even though there would be no discernable time differential by mailing only. Plus they request that you waste your time and reply by fax, e-mail (another machine) or phone to confirm when you received their fax. When the mailed papers do arrive, it is clearly stated that only the original papers are acceptable with original signatures, which begs the question "Why was the material faxed in the first place?" Was the fax meant to forewarn you that something was coming? Most people don't await with anticipation the coming of what should be routine paperwork. Maybe that's the whole point. Maybe the sender of the duplicates has heightened the sense of their importance and thereby his or her own importance.

Then there's the inexplicable attraction for the copier. When simple directions ask that one copy be retained by receiver and the second be returned to sender, it is remarkable how often both copies are sent back. Was this an oversight or did the recipient give in to the lure of a copier? Did the receiver succumb to the desire to make his/her own copies, even when they would be superfluous? Since you do not know, you must waste more time resending the papers that should not have been sent back to you in the first place.

Next the perpetrator spies the stamp machine, which must prove irresistible. More than one employee, I would venture to guess, has assumed that one or two of what would be considered personal correspondence could be passed through the office stamp machine without being noticed. I believe machines should simplify ones' paperwork, not tempt ones' soul.

I ONLY HAVE TROUBLE WITH PEOPLE…

…who don't pray. My idea of prayer is a "thank you." I truly like all those "Hallelujah" choruses. As a child, I was always impressed by the entrance of the pastor of The Peoples' Church of Chicago, Dr. Preston Bradley, as he solemnly strode onto the dais each Sunday to begin the service. The music went something like this: "Praise him from whom all blessings flow; praise him all creatures here below; praise him …da..da..da..da.da.da; praise …da..da..da..da..da..da..da." Remember I was just an impressionable child at the time, so I guess I should try to find out the correct lyrics. But this is the way I remember them. And that to me is what it's all about. If your mind is focused on the positive with words of praise or thanksgiving, if you are able to bring some elevated thinking into your life and concentrate on that for a few minutes each day, if you can open a window to optimism and hope and if you can just send all those good vibes out into the universe, it can't hurt.

I ONLY HAVE TROUBLE WITH PEOPLE...

...who don't read newspapers. No one seems to have time anymore. But for anyone to think they are being fully informed by catching bits of TV news, TV late night shows, radio shows or blogs, they are fooling themselves and should not be allowed to participate in any attempt at rational discussion of world events. Needless to say they shouldn't be allowed to vote. Most newspapers have the resources to relate issues with some depth and analysis. The newspaper reader has to devote some of his/her precious time to digest the material. The reader has to focus his attention in a more concentrated manner. The reader's attention is not divided. The reader's bias or pre-conceived notions are not necessarily being reaffirmed. The reader is not actively thinking how to respond to the ideas coming his way. The newspaper reader is probably a very interesting person.

I ONLY HAVE TROUBLE WITH PEOPLE…

…who can't sit still. Now I'm not talking about kids, those bundles of kinetic energy. I'm talking about adults. Adults at the movies. Adults in a theatre audience. Specifically the adult seated in front of me. Usually a person leans to one side or the other and remains in that general position, perhaps preferring the right or left armrest, the one with or without the cup holder? The person behind can adjust and obtain a clear, unobstructed view of the stage or screen. But when someone cannot sit still, when a person shifts left to right, right to left, back to front, front to back in their seat, the person behind has a hard, practically impossible, time focusing on the entertainment. In a movie theatre, generally you can change seats, interrupting the continuity of your viewing, but getting rid of the larger problem. But in a "theatre" theatre, your ticket has a number on it. You're there to see a "live" performance. Too bad if it's the one taking place in the row in front of you.

I ONLY HAVE TROUBLE WITH PEOPLE…

…who support girls only / boys only soccer. I love soccer. I love that so many five year olds and up play this team sport, but I do not like segregated teams for the youngest participants. Years ago, I was commissioner for an AYSO (American Youth Soccer Organization) region in Chicago. The average elementary school family was just starting to become aware of the world-renowned sport. As a fledgling organization, we spent an inordinate amount of time selling the program and educating the public that there was an alternative to ballet lessons and little league baseball. Luckily we had adults who were willing to learn about the sport and being smack in the center of a multicultural metropolis, we had the expertise of fathers who really played and knew the game. It took a few years for the game to take hold. During that time it was only common sense, in order to provide enough competition, for the teams whose players ranged from kindergarten through eighth grade, to be composed of both boys and girls. We had coed soccer…an equal opportunity sport. Revolutionary!

Interestingly, in the youngest years, the girls often surpassed the boys in attention span (the tales of daisy pickers were legendary) and understanding of the game itself (basically, movement of the ball down the field away from ones' own goal and into the other). I'd say as far as coordination was concerned, the two sexes were evenly matched. There were some kids whose athletic talents were already in evidence at the earliest levels. Of course, there were always those whose only athletic trophies would be for attendance.

As they grew older the human playing field did not remain level. Boys, due to their seemingly natural aggressiveness, physical strength, speed and stamina often outperformed their feminine teammates. But therein lies the point. They were still teammates. They practiced together. They worked out together. They played together. They communicated with each other and they had fun together. I don't know of anything else comparable to that kind of preteen experience.

Sadly, as far as I'm concerned, the "Powers that Be" decided the teams must be segregated, under the guise "Girls' skills would improve. They'd get more touches." Isn't that what practices are for? We're not interested in creating international superstars.

    Underlying the rational for separate teams was "more girls would participate, because the weaker sex is having difficulty coping with the pressures of competition in a masculine dominated arena." I believe there is plenty of time during high school, college and adulthood, if the athlete is so inclined, to play on one sex teams. At those levels, the focus is more intense and the commitment is more defined. I just can't understand why at the very beginning of our children's socialization, they are being taught, subconsciously, the sexes are not equal. Youth soccer had the golden opportunity to level the playing field. Instead it scored an "own goal."

I ONLY HAVE TROUBLE WITH PEOPLE…

…who keep up with their reading. With all the information sources available these days, I don't understand how anyone can possibly honestly say they have this part of their lives under control. If I enter a person's home and don't see stacks of newspapers and piles of magazines, I begin to wonder. I guess if you simply skim the daily papers and have the discipline not to subscribe to many magazines, that could be a satisfactory explanation. Of course, the plain truth could be you don't read newspapers and don't subscribe to any magazines. Oh dear. Surely, there are bookshelves and they are filled with books, rather than knickknacks and plants. Is it really believable that someone has read every single one of their books? Well, say that they have. There are many, many more in bookstores. I doubt anyone could browse through the aisles and not find something to add to their collection.

Assuming they have the resources, does anyone ever get to the point where they say, "I have enough books?" If the problem is space, books are always welcome donations. Friends often swap. Some books become friends and therefore cannot be supplanted. So what are we dealing with here? Somebody who does not read newspapers or reads them faithfully each day and tosses them the next. Somebody who does not oversubscribe to magazines and manages to find time to keep up weekly or monthly. And somebody who has read every book he/she owns, cannot part with a single one and has no place to house any more. That to me is the only kind of person who has kept up with their reading. That to me is strange.

I ONLY HAVE TROUBLE WITH PEOPLE...

...who won't eat anything fattening. First of all, everything can be fattening, if you eat enough of it. I'll admit though, some foods are more fattening than others. But the person who won't eat that tempting dessert is just trying to be a spoilsport. The non-partaker is just trying to make the partaker feel guilty. Anyone who has been on a diet, even those who have successfully lost weight, knows you cannot remain on that particular diet for the rest of your life. And if you can't, it follows that your ideal weight is not going to be retained. There has to be a calculation about what foods that have been denied can be selectively reintroduced into your daily or weekly life. In my personal case, I lost twenty- five pounds by eliminating most carbohydrates and severely limiting dairy and alcoholic products. While I was in the process of losing the pounds, I always thought it would be foolish not to drink any orange juice or brandy, because I knew as soon as I attained my "ideal" weight, I would go back to a normal breakfast and cocktail hour. Likewise, I couldn't accept the fact that one should only eat chicken breasts. I really don't like white meat, no matter what you do to it. I'm a leg and thigh girl.

I found it nonsensical to follow a plan that was not at all aligned with my taste buds. So I went about "dieting" without sacrificing everything enjoyable about feeding my face. When the scale got to where I wanted it to be, I gradually started reintroducing favorites. There are foods I know I can add without jumping three to five pounds in a day. Unfortunately, pizza and pasta are not two of those, at least for me. This does not mean I can never indulge, but it does mean I need to watch what I eat the next few days. I no longer eat potatoes or rice or bread everyday, but my body doesn't seem to mind a little ice cream each evening. Each person needs to evaluate their particular, individual reactions. There are foods I would never eat more than once a month. But that "never" doesn't mean never. I guess I'm just trying to say, when it comes to food, you CAN have it all.

I ONLY HAVE TROUBLE WITH PEOPLE…

…who make Saturday Night Live sketches into movies. Okay, they may be good for a few laughs. But SNL is free and, need I remind you, movies are not? I think the public deserves better. Though the way they flock to this fluff, they may not think so themselves. Unless the audience stops supporting mediocrity, there is no incentive for comedians to stretch. And I don't mean just stretching sketches out to 2 hours of playing time. We can all understand the megalomaniac urge to reach the widest amount of the population and to make a lot of money. Did the comedian dumb down to please the lowest denominator or is this the best he or she has to offer? Does the consumer find comfort in seeing the same old thing over and over again or does he or she realize that surprise is a necessary ingredient of humor? Do we have a choice? "Which came first? The chicken or the egg?" Who should be the leader? Who should be the follower? The comic or the consumer?

I ONLY HAVE TROUBLE WITH PEOPLE…

…who use digital cameras. With a digital camera, if the shooter doesn't like the picture, it can easily be erased. When using a regular camera, the photographer has to endure the time period to shoot the entire roll of film, take the film in to be developed, wait the appropriate number of days and often face a terrible reality. The photographer must confront the fact that either he/she is guilty of poor judgment or lack of talent. Perhaps the chosen subjects were not in focus or in the center of the picture. You see red-eyed people who were not drunk at that particular time. Blurry pictures that are indecipherable, implying the photographer had the shakes. Downright unattractive poses or expressions that must be destroyed for the sake of everyone involved. The photographer with the digital camera avoids all those pitfalls. He doesn't have to make the difficult decisions. " Do I toss these in the wastepaper basket or do I place them in the photo album for posterity?" "Will the subjects be big enough to laugh at themselves or will they view this display as a betrayal?" Oh, digital camera owners, I have a flash for you. You are avoiding major moral issues. You are behaving like paparazzi.

I ONLY HAVE TROUBLE WITH PEOPLE...

...who scroll. This is rather a new phenomenon. Often at the bottom of your television screen, there will be messages, most often updated news items. This is disturbing to me. If on-screen action is the purpose of the telecast, which I imagine is the only reason to be broadcasting in the first place, scrolling is at best a distraction. The viewers' attention is divided and who is that supposed to benefit? Perhaps if the scroll is offering a service to the viewer it would be excusable. What if during a discussion or debate the scroll could identify truth from fiction? Who is lying, who is fantasizing, who is on the level? There should be a way to signify such without using words. Unlike scrolling, the message could be more subtle.

Maybe we could adopt a technique from the universal world of soccer. When fouls are committed, the referee may allow play to continue (advantage), he may issue a yellow card (caution) or a red card (ejection). It all depends on the seriousness of the offense.

In soccer, generally when something looks like a foul, it usually is a foul. In the world of television talk, it is not so obvious. Imagine this on the bottom of your screen. When so-called pundits speak "truth," nothing happens. When they "spin" or misrepresent the facts, a yellow card appears on the bottom of the picture. When they out and out "lie," a red card is whipped out for all to see. If this program were in place, perhaps we'd find that less and less cards would need to be issued. Who, you may ask, would act as the referee in such a format? The networks themselves wouldn't want to critique the responses of their guests. Referees are often perceived as the "villain." Their skills vary, their judgments too. No matter how well trained or intelligent, no matter how well versed on the subject, mistakes will be made. Certain networks might have to be yellow or red carded themselves. But it wouldn't matter. Just show me the cards. Unlike a basketball or hockey game, where your disagreement with the professional ref makes no difference in the outcome, YOU would be making the final call.

I ONLY HAVE TROUBLE WITH PEOPLE...

...who are silent fathers. I think there are some myths about fathers that should be debunked. Those strong, silent movie heroes do not transfer well from reel to real life. Why should fathers feel they are not really necessary in those first few months of an infant's life? The baby only needs its mother in the beginning? Doesn't "bringing home the bacon" imply you must be home at some time? Do the fewer moments spent with family increase the momentousness of those occasions to an unrealistic degree? Is the idolatry of the father ensured by his absence? Is the power of his words heightened by their scarcity? I'm just asking. I really don't know, because I had a very communicative, talkative father, whose personality and presence were quite exceptional. This had not come naturally to him. I was told he was a terribly shy person long into his young adulthood. He blushed... a lot. He studied Public Speaking at night school. He believed in his grammar school motto, "Perseverance Leads To Progress."

He had a charisma that seemed to be attractive to all he met, so he certainly had a profound impression on me. I was the lucky one who got to spend the most time with him. I felt special, simply having him for a father. All right, he didn't talk all the time, like when he was scratching my back. Like when we were ice skating, twirling around the frozen pond, arms linked, doing our own Olympics dancing. Like when we were polkaing, but then we were laughing and singing. With my childhood being what it was, it should be obvious, my children's father is also not a mime.

I ONLY HAVE TROUBLE WITH PEOPLE…

…who frown on the word "liberal." Let's honestly face the simple fact that America is a liberal country. Some people say they are conservative. They use that term, I think unadvisedly, as the opposite, the antonym of liberal. Yet when speaking about the United States of America that cannot apply. You could be a conservative liberal versus a liberal liberal. But you are still a liberal, because, as defined in Webster's New Collegiate Dictionary, its' meaning is "having tendency toward democratic or republican, as distinguished from monarchial or aristocratic, forms." I believe that applies to citizens of this country…ALL THE CITIZENS.

As an afterthought, if some fear being associated with the definition " Free from restraint; unchecked; licentious i.e. lawless, lewd," realize that that definition for the word liberal is "Archaic."

I ONLY HAVE TROUBLE WITH PEOPLE...

...who think higher is better. I recently attended a truly lovely wedding at which the soloist unfortunately applied this notion to her singing of the Lord's Prayer. There were a few screechingly uncomfortable moments because of it. As a former high-rise dweller, panoramic views become dimmer from the 29th floor when the elevators are out of order. Some may think the higher the price the better the quality of merchandise, until it comes to gas prices. Consider the racehorse that comes out of the gate at high speed, but can't sustain it for the 7 furlongs. An automobile has no problem maintaining high speed until the cop car catches up. Most prefer the higher temperatures of the spring and summer months or southern climes, but most are becoming aware of this thing called Global Warming. Naturally when thinking of those who believe "higher is better," partygoers, hearty partygoers, come to mind. If one drink makes me feel good, how about another and another and another? Still feeling better? I really can't speak to those whose preferred means of intoxication are stronger than alcohol. I can't speak to that kind of high, because I don't understand it. But then again, they probably wouldn't listen to me anyway.

I ONLY HAVE TROUBLE WITH PEOPLE…

…who don't frequent live theatre. I'm not including rock concerts. I'm not including mosh pits. Comedy clubs do not count. I'm referring to a production which involves a playwright, a director and a cast. Money is not an excuse. Unless a person is in dire straits, people find means to go to the movies. Besides you can often find plays that are FREE!

Maybe it takes a little more effort to attend live theatre. After all, it does take a bit more advance planning. You have a limited choice of showings. You can't just spontaneously show up at the box office sure to find something that meets with your timetable. You may have to eat and drink something before showtime. It's a rare theatre which encourages purchasing humungous boxes of popcorn just prior to the performance. In fact, an announcement could be made to kindly unwrap your throat lozenges before the curtain goes up.

You also need to arrive on time. There will not be dozens of previews to cover up for your tardiness. Actually, you will probably receive nasty looks from the patrons you disturb while getting to your seat.

Then you will be expected to pay attention to the proceedings. There is certainly more dialogue to follow. And you don't have the prerogative to have a brain cramp during extended "action" scenes. You can't just sit back. This is truly an interactive experience. Those actors on stage are not performing in a vacuum . They are relying on you for your feedback, whether that be laughter, applause or appreciative silence.

Maybe the phrase "frequent live theatre" is a poor choice of words. Unless you're an actor, you're not going to go to the theatre as often as you would the movies. Which would make theatre-going, may I say, more special. Indeed it is. A play is a one time only event. A theatrical experience can never be the same. It is live in real time. Hopefully, you'll be there.

I ONLY HAVE TROUBLE WITH PEOPLE…

…who don't worry about things. One of the distinct differences between humans and other animals is that we have the capacity for fretting and they don't. I think we should be proud of that distinguishing characteristic. You often hear people rhapsodize about the unconditional love they receive from their pets. Humans, on the other hand, pick the petals off flowers, wondering " He loves me. She loves me not." What would "the course of true love" be if it indeed "did run smooth?" Who wants to argue with Shakespeare? I believe half the job of parenthood is worrying, because what else could you be doing that could be more important when your children are out on their own, no longer under your surveillance? Afterwards, there is the reward you receive when your worst fears do not come true. What relief! What joy! Nothing else quite compares. What causes you to visit your doctor or dentist or ophthalmologist? Why do you have the good intentions of watching your weight, exercising or curbing destructive habits? We are creatures of conscientious consciousness. To borrow from Erma Bombeck, WORRY: "it's the gift that keeps on giving."

I ONLY HAVE TROUBLE WITH PEOPLE…

…who have no wedding manners. I strongly feel that, though the marriage ceremony and celebration should be one of joy, there is a serious step being taken here. One that should have a degree of solemnity and decorum. I guess for some, the dancing, the music, the toasting, the dining, the drinking are not sufficient to meet their definition of a "Good Time." Some brides and grooms just can't resist the urge to smash a piece of wedding cake in each other's face. I don't get it. After all, these would be the same people who, or whose parents, spent mucho money on wedding apparel, hair dressers, make-up, etc. to which end the couple would appear to the world as close to perfection as possible. They would have devoted hours and hours to making decisions about their appearance, then hours on the actual preparation and presentation. Now, within a few seconds, they look like clowns, hit with a whipped cream pie. Worse than looking like clowns is looking like asses. Literally and figuratively. This happens when members of the wedding party "moon" the bride and groom, as the newlyweds and unsuspecting guests depart the celebration. What Hilarity! Somewhere, somehow, some people never quite leave adolescence behind. I would think a wedding would be a good place to take that first step.

I ONLY HAVE TROUBLE WITH PEOPLE...

...who don't prioritize. Most people, I assume, have many demands on their time. Some of these demands are not amenable to personal choice. Unless you are self-employed, your work schedule is out of your control. If your children rely on you for transportation, the timetable of their activities, from school to extra curriculars, may structure the majority of your day.
Therefore, I would think it a necessity to plan for the hours that are at your disposal to do as you will. But what would that be? The possibilities could be endless. Including endless chores. When does doing laundry take precedence? After a single day, a couple of days, a week? A month? I wouldn't go there. How about house cleaning? Is it time to straighten up, lightly vacuum and feather dust, or is this a move- the- furniture and wash- the- walls major cleansing? When it involves dirty dishes and the Health and Sanitation Department, most, I feel, would move that duty further up on the list of priorities. On the other hand, time can be well spent doing what some would call "Nothing." Reading, watching TV, seeing a movie, visiting with friends, soaking in the tub, having a massage, playing a game, probably, are either too prominent or too lacking in everyday life.

Then just how do such things as eating, exercising and sleeping fit in? I consider these activities as necessities, but they can greatly vary in the actual amount of time devoted to them. Are you going to spend time in preparation of a meal or two or three? Are you going to actually sit down to eat and enjoy it? Are you really going to exercise actively from thirty to forty to sixty minutes daily or maybe five times a week as recommended by fitness experts or does just contemplating that thought make you break a sweat? There doesn't even seem to be a consensus of whether six or eight hours of sleep at night is needed to function at optimum level. Your own body would be your best guide if you're not too tired to trust it. Parents of newborn infants don't stand a chance.

Despite personal desires, you'll still have to coordinate with others. For your own well being, it would be best to come to the table with some priorities in place, some thoughts of your own, so as not to be left to the mercy of the more vociferous. It's no wonder that many feel as if they're running in circles, if not in place. They feel that they have lost control of their lives. They have too many balls in the air and they failed juggling in clown school. Figure out what's important to you and don't drop the ball.

I ONLY HAVE TROUBLE WITH PEOPLE...

...who talk when you're talking to someone else on the telephone. Maybe the person has something to offer to the conversation. Maybe the person feels left out. Maybe the person feels you are not expressing yourself coherently. They're just trying to help. Maybe you should just hand the phone over. However, that might irritate the caller. If the caller had wanted to talk to someone else, I would think that's the person they would have called in the first place. Sometimes the culprit is talking about something entirely different. Maybe the person doesn't realize you are on the phone. Your hair could be hiding the receiver. You could say, "Excuse me. I'm on the phone right now." If it were indeed an emergency, the "phonee" could tell the "phoner," "Let me call you back." But, I would bet, ninety-nine percent of the time, the "phonee" would be calling right back immediately, saying, "Oh, it was nothing." Maybe the person wants to make a call. Maybe the person is expecting a call and his/her purpose is to get you off the phone. This now has turned into a whole territorial thing. The supremacy of the sound waves. The dominance of the telephone wires. This is much more serious than the mere inconsideration of a "butter-inner." This is a power grab. Beware.

I ONLY HAVE TROUBLE WITH PEOPLE...

...who take babies on long airplane trips.

Tell your own story:

(Feel free to use the blank pages at the back of the book if more space is needed.)

I ONLY HAVE TROUBLE WITH PEOPLE...

...who blame God. There have been more natural disasters and man-made catastrophes, unfortunately, as of late. There have been attempts to understand these misfortunes by explaining them as punishments for our sins or as cosmic tests to challenge our resolve. We may need to rationalize what we, at this point in time, can't understand. But why bring God into it? Isn't that the easy way out? Are we so weak that we can't face facts and move forward? But if we are so weak, and if one thinks we were created in God's image, what does that say about God?

I concede there may be a need to pray for guidance. But if God is punishing or testing us, why would God now, after the fact, offer assistance? In the aftermath of tragedy, the outpouring of love, caring and good will can be a powerful force toward the betterment of mankind. We need not be fatalists. We need not have a vengeful, hateful God.

I ONLY HAVE TROUBLE WITH PEOPLE...

...who don't know how to cheer. I don't know when it all started, but somehow all new scoreboards, whether for baseball or basketball, do way more than keep the stadium fans aware of the score. They are now concrete, square or rectangular, electronic CHEERLEADERS. They don't just offer prompts. They tell the spectators the exact words to yell and they tell them when to yell them. They organize and start the WAVE. What used to be a spontaneous, though I feel unnecessary, exercise is now completely artificial.

   I may have mentioned previously that I have been a lifelong Cubbie fan. I sincerely believe in the power of the "tenth player" in the stands. That that electricity can morph into a positive outcome for your team. Wrigley Field fans never had to be prodded to actively engage in the game. They could just as easily be standing and applauding in the top of the first as their pitcher delivers the 2 out 3 & 2 pitch as they would in the ninth with a slim one run lead as their pitcher delivers the 2 out 3 & 2 pitch with the bases loaded...the game on the line.

But maybe this kind of impulsive energy can be misconstrued. My questions is, "Can the powers that be distinguish whether the fans are rooting for the pitcher or the batter?" Could it be that the fans don't even know what they're cheering for? If there is no difference between responses whether it be in the first or the ninth inning, I believe this is what could be the problem at Wrigley. This could be the reason the Cubs haven't been to the World Series in sixty odd years.

   Does this lend support for those cheerleader scoreboards? Heaven forbid.

I ONLY HAVE TROUBLE WITH PEOPLE...

...who misuse data. Numbers can be confusing enough, but when people cherry pick the statistics they present to prove their point, support their position and refute their opposition, the average reader or consumer is not being well informed. A case in point is the use of such words as average, median and mean. Dictionary definitions do not necessarily help matters. Average: An arithmetic mean. Median: Designating the middle point in a series of values. Mean: A number contained within the range of a set of numbers and representative of each of the set. For example: 8 is the median of 2,5,8,10, 13. Whereas the mean would be 19. One would add the integers and divide by 2. Such a difference strikes me when tax relief is discussed. The tax reductions for the middle class seem to be greatly increased when finding the mean for tax cuts ranging from $2000 to $13,000, which would be $5,500. But that is not factual, because the lowest earner is not getting a $5,500 break. This earner is still receiving just $2000. Am I making any "cents?"

I ONLY HAVE TROUBLE WITH PEOPLE...

...who swear around young and old people. I consider myself old enough not to be sworn around. I understand that times have changed. The general culture seems more crass than I remember earlier in my lifetime. It's probably better to be a more permissive society, than a few seemingly short years ago, when Lenny Bruce could be persecuted for using foul language. There certainly are places, such as comedy clubs, locker rooms, where honest communication probably would not be possible without four-letter words. However, I guess I expect people to be aware of where they are, adjust to their surroundings and have some consideration for others. That would include not offending families by subjecting their children to raw language, say, at a baseball game. I feel sorry for grannies and grandpas, who are hard of hearing. The poor dears are straining to understand what someone is saying, only to be left with their ears burning. Maybe when all of society becomes immune to cursing, the perpetrators will desist. They'll probably find another way to offend though. It's amazing how creative some people can be.

I ONLY HAVE TROUBLE WITH PEOPLE...

...who don't smile when their picture is being taken. Everyone has seen those formal family photographs from the late 1800's and early 1900's. Each subject sits grimly with stiff posture and starched clothes. Perhaps during difficult times and wearing uncomfortable clothes their frozen, serious expressions could be forgiven. But there are some folks still today, who do not respond to such cues as " Say cheese", "Smile" or "Pizza." I'm not talking about people who are caught off guard, who just didn't know what turned out to be a terrible picture was happening. They didn't mean to look that way. They are innocent, even though ugly. I think everybody, and I mean EVERYBODY, looks better when they smile. This is not a secret. How could it be... to anyone? What puzzles me is what kind of perversity is it that someone wouldn't want to look his or her best when being photographed? Is this an odd show of snobbery? " Really, all this foolishness is beneath me." I hate to assign deceitful motivations to people. Maybe the " not- able- to- smile- for- picture- taking" humans are just hard of hearing.

I ONLY HAVE TROUBLE WITH PEOPLE…

…who debunk astrology. I doubt if there has ever been a more overused pick-up line than "What's your sign?" which, by the way, works. I would also suggest, that though not a faithful daily horoscope reader, if you happen upon the page on which it is printed, you would be mighty tempted to read yours. There has to be a reason newspapers and magazines carry these columns. They are not in the business of wasting space. Not long ago, people knew the names of the top astrologers. Sydney Omarr, Jeanne Dixon and Carroll Righter were celebrities in and of themselves. That time has passed, as have they, I'm afraid. But the guilty desire to know the future is alive and thriving in film and literature of all kinds.

I admit I read the daily horoscope, but for amusement, not insight. I do, however, take seriously astrological character analyses. For instance, I have never met a Gemini without a sense of humor nor a Scorpio who lays all their cards on the table. You may argue the traits are too general. Everyone has a sense of humor or secrecy. It's a case of degree. Some qualities are more pronounced, or less so, in the twelve signs of the Zodiac. A clearer picture emerges if one knows the rising sign as well as the sun and moon signs.

I always found the following two facts interesting. The ebb and flow of the ocean tides are caused by the sun and moon and the human body is two-thirds water. Ergo, the sun and moon could feasibly pull humans in one direction or another, could they not? As Shakespeare wrote, " The fault, dear Brutus, is not in our stars, but in ourselves." He said nothing about the <u>sun</u> and the <u>moon</u>.

I ONLY HAVE TROUBLE WITH PEOPLE...

...who misuse the word "elite." Somehow, though intentionally, one political party has been sneeringly designated as elitist. Yet I don't believe the term is the exclusive property of a singular government philosophy. Most often social superiority of the elite is determined by money and in fact, the greater wealth lies with the opposite party. The difference in the TWO branches of the governing elites is how that money is used. Is it spread by legislation among the population for the overall benefit of the society? Or is it held close by the few?

I ONLY HAVE TROUBLE WITH PEOPLE...

...who don't teach their children how to behave poolside. A pool is not a bathtub. Whatever playtime is like in ones' own bathroom is nobody's business. However, splashing and thrashing about in a public pool should not be encouraged unless one is drowning. Likewise for screaming. There are matters of life and death for which I will make allowances. Behavior that is poor when not in a pool does not all of a sudden become acceptable when in a pool. Siblings hitting or pushing each other is a case in point. I find pummeling is no better an activity with or without water. I also don't understand parents who don't seem to mind watching their little ones run around the wet, slick and slippery deck. I don't know, but I never thought my kids were injury-proof. Accidents do happen. There's no reason to try to defy gravity. Kids do fall. They do get hurt. They do wail. Why wouldn't a parent want to avoid a trip to the emergency room? Then there's peeing in the pool...I'm not even going to go there.

I ONLY HAVE TROUBLE WITH PEOPLE...

...who do not think being cheap is a virtue. I am a Bohemian and proud of it. Oh, not the artsy Greenwich Village kind, but genetically, ancestrally of Bohemia, specifically Prague, Czechoslovakia. Growing up, I remember that family related stories dealt mainly with two themes. Number One was houbies. Houbies are mushrooms. Supposedly, Bohemians spend a lot of time hunting for houbies. Still to this day, there are parades celebrating the houby. The second legendary story line (and I remember some of my relatives doing this, whereas I don't remember any actually houby hunting) was living in the basement, so you could rent out the upper floors of your house. Now that to me is the epitome of being cheap. Yet I'm still proud to be a Bohemian. So people who hit the "Sales," people who love bargains, people who clip coupons, people who always ask for a doggy bag who don't own a dog, people who welcome hand-me-downs, people who traffic thrift shops, consider yourself "Family." Unless, of course, you don't tip.

I ONLY HAVE TROUBLE WITH PEOPLE...

...who are against gun regulations. I have a hard time believing that reasonable people can't negotiate a sensible policy on guns in our society. If we were to apply the rationale that " Guns don't kill. People do" to cars, i.e. " Cars don't kill. People do," that would lead us to believe that cars should not have licensed drivers. Cars should not be registered. But they are.

We register voters. We register both births and deaths. We license marriages. We license businesses. Registration and licensing of people does not seem to threaten those rights. Right, right?

I ONLY HAVE TROUBLE WITH PEOPLE…

…who tease children. The younger the child the worse the offense. Genuine laughter brought on by tickling can easily cross the line into pain. Blowing a raspberry on that tiny belly is another innocent act that can lead to unintended consequences. It's up to the parent not to get carried away with the moment and realize when the tone of the giggles has changed. I even think that peek-a-boo can go to the extreme. The idea is the child believes you have all of a sudden disappeared and then magically you reappear just by removing your hands. I think the child who is subjected to this "game" may not be too pleased with the insubstantiality of this relationship. When the child is old enough to remove the adult's hands himself, thereby having some control over the situation, teasing can be avoided.

Perhaps the biggest tease of all is Santa Claus. It's no wonder so many parents have such a traumatic time of it when they have to face their children with reality one day. I really don't think it is necessary to make Santa the be all and end all in order to fully enjoy Christmas. Even if Santa is just one of the present givers, along with Mom and Dad, siblings, grandparents, aunts and uncles, etc., he would still have a special place. None of the others, I presume, wears a bright red suit and rides in a sleigh drawn by eight reindeer. As with all manner of teasing, it's the excessiveness of the concentrated activity that causes the situation to get out of hand, leading to downright unpleasantness.

Cool it.

I ONLY HAVE TROUBLE WITH PEOPLE...

...who must always do something. I think it's rather common that when someone tells you their problem they just want to vent. In fact, they often become more aggravated when offered advice or help of any kind. I've never been to a psychiatrist or a psychologist, but from what I can glean from movies or television, they follow a pattern of mirroring. They just repeat what their patient is saying. They allow the patient to take the lead on the road to self-awareness. I think this is something most doctors simply don't understand.

Someday, maybe this is just wishful thinking, but I'd like, after having undergone the annual physical, to hear the GP say, " Everything seems just fine." Of course, if there is a problem, I want to hear about it. In detail. I don't want to be lied to and have to sue somebody. But there always seems to be... "Well, we could do this. We could try such and such. Your insurance probably would pay for the test." Patients must be expecting their physicians to do something, even though that cold is just going to have to run its course. So what's the poor Doc to do? There's also proactive dentistry. There may be no warning signs, no pain, no sensitivity. But a filling could be composed of a material found wanting or it's going to have to be replaced... someday. Why not NOW? I think this is another "Cool it."

I ONLY HAVE TROUBLE WITH PEOPLE…

…who buy into stereotypes. There was a time when you could always tell the bad guys from the good guys. The good guys wore white hats. Then along came Hopalong Cassidy…the good guy in the black cowboy hat. That was over fifty some years ago when he upended the generally conventional image. I guess, some things don't progress in a linear manner, thereby getting better with the passage of time. No, today we have red states and blue states. Instead of eliminating stereotypes, they have been expanded… to include EVERYBODY. Whose brilliant idea was that? Half of the nation presumably loves God, guns and the unborn, while the other loves taxes, governmental spending and X-rated movies. Half of the population hates minorities, the poor and gays, while the other hates Christmas, the second amendment and the military. It doesn't seem to matter that these characterizations are basically untrue. I would hope they don't exist at all…in any one individual, let alone, in a group of people. Yet this stereotypical thinking seems to have become more commonplace. Stereotypes need not be completely obliterated from our culture…not that they ever could be. But they have their place. In cartoons.

I ONLY HAVE TROUBLE WITH PEOPLE…

…who don't have a passion. I don't think living passionately is the same thing as having a passion. Those who live passionately probably wear themselves out rather quickly. Living passionately would imply a consistently exhaustive state. In fact, I would expect to find a passion to ebb and flow throughout one's life. And I don't expect people to be driven by necessarily the same passion throughout their lives. A passion could come about unexpectedly. You become aware of something missing. You could be called upon to create something to fulfill a void. The act of creating in itself is what drives artists, musicians, actors, writers. But that "let's get it on" attitude is not theirs alone. Anyone, if they have their antennae up, should be able to recognize an opportunity to become intensely involved. There are many, many "so called causes" that could stir ones' passion…charities, politics, community service, education, health care, child or elder care.

Things don't have to be the way they have always been. There will always be room for invention, new ideas, originality. Volunteers have a passion. They are the lucky ones.

I ONLY HAVE TROUBLE WITH PEOPLE...

...who don't care how they appear to others. People don't have to look at themselves unless they want to. Others are not so fortunate. Males may feel comfortable when unshaven, but that 5 o'clock shadow makes me feel itchy. Women with curlers in their hair may think it of little consequence, but really, this truly inhuman look should be confined by law to beauty shops, where everyone is suffering the same humiliation. Sadly, the people who are in the closest relationships are the worst perpetrators. Why should the ones we care about the most have to see each other brush their teeth? Open mouths oozing foamy toothpaste is not a pleasant sight. Sharing everything is not always for the best. Males sitting, watching TV, in their underwear, with beer bellies hanging over shouldn't think they're cute. I'm not saying that women should emulate the stereotype of the fifties and do housework in heels and frilly dresses, but likewise the stereotype of the wife wrapped in a tattered housecoat is not an inviting picture.

As men get older they may lose hair on top of their heads, but it seems they gain hair in their ears and noses. There are inexpensive grooming aids that can be of assistance here. Older women, perhaps because of diminishing eyesight, often overdo it with the makeup. Wild blue eye shadow. Bright red bow-shaped lips. There may a line that shouldn't be crossed. Start with the lip line.

I ONLY HAVE TROUBLE WITH PEOPLE…

…who don't like to play games. There are so many kinds of games to choose from that it makes it difficult to defend someone who prefers to sit on the sidelines. If I invited you to my home, I'd offer a variety of board games…oldies, but goodies like CLUE, LIFE. I also have all sorts of trivia games. Then there's always card games from UNO to TEXAS HOLD 'EM. Some games may require actually getting up off your chair, CHARADES being my all time favorite. Games can challenge in a number of different ways. I think you can tell an awful lot about a person's personality from the manner in which they play games.

Maybe that's what the non-participant is afraid of. The player may have to depend on his/her intelligence, memory, quick thinking ability, deductive reasoning or just plain luck. But what do you really have to lose? Except maybe in TEXAS HOLD 'EM. But then just don't buy in again after you lose your first wad. Maybe the non-participant has subconscious memories of bad childhood experiences at birthday parties.

I always disliked those games of "exclusion," MUSICAL CHAIRS being the Number 1 offender. Imagine you're the first kid out. You have to stand on the outskirts for what must seem like eternity, while all the other kids get to race around to the music, laughing and grimacing, not missing you one iota. The fact that soon other kids will be joining you makes no difference. You're all losers. Live with it.

There also are the children games of "embarrassment." I suggest "PIN THE TAIL ON THE DONKEY" is one of these culprits. Wherever you may pin that tail, it most assuredly will not be near where the tail should be. There it is, in plain sight for all to see. You do not know where an ass' ass is. And that makes you…? I hope these games are no longer party staples. I hope they haven't ruined the psyches of too many future game players. Adults need people to play with too.

I ONLY HAVE TROUBLE WITH PEOPLE…

…who crowd the airport baggage carousel.
The comments are uncommonly universal.
 "Excuse me…EXCUSE ME!"
 " Grab that bag…yes, the red one."
"THAT'S MY BAG!"
"OH, I'm sorry…are you okay?"
 " Excuse me…EXCUSE ME!"

 Everyone just please take two giant steps backward… away from the carousel.   Ah…now we can all see and retrieve our luggage…as the merry-go-round passes by. Voila!

I ONLY HAVE TROUBLE WITH PEOPLE…

…who constantly win at the race track. Yes, those people who play the ponies and actually collect money at the end of a race! Hours are spent by handicappers, both professional and amateur, analyzing data about owners, trainers, race history, tracks, distance, surface (turf or dirt), weights, sires, mares, equipment, blinkers, jockeys (who's hot?) etcetera, etcetera, etcetera. There's a certain pride to be had from the ability to read and interpret The Racing Form. An added pleasure in being aware of insider minutia. Yet, 99% of these race track junkies (myself included) find very little money in their pockets at the end of the day. But the bettors who pick by name …number…colors (horse or jockey silks)…the cutest jockey… They WIN! They have all the luck and all the money. How do they do that? They don't have a clue. Their innocence is almost universal and unbearable. They just WIN! They have a gift? Oh, PLEASE. I'm so jealous and so broke.

I ONLY HAVE TROUBLE WITH PEOPLE…

…who are pseudo scientists. I find it disturbing that we have been revisiting the Scopes Trial. We have returned to 1925. What progress! We have Americans who believe that man walked on earth with the dinosaurs. My God, they must have taken the movie "King Kong" literally. The arrogance of adults and students who pressure school boards and teachers to impugn their expertise is weakening the quality of education for all. Similarly, these pseudo scientists can see into the future with as much certainty as they can reveal the secrets of the ancient past. They flatly state there is no such thing as global warming, that there is no reason to pursue a course at the present time that would emphasize the need to protect the environment. We needn't concern ourselves with clean air or clean water. No, because that's <u>real</u> science.

I ONLY HAVE TROUBLE WITH PEOPLE...

...who wave things at basketball games. There is this, I feel, strangely rude behavior that takes place when the opposing team is at the free throw line. The fans of the home team stand and wave these foam noodles, or whatever, supposedly to divert the shooter. I would assume the professional basketball player could focus his attention and block out these distractions. But I don't think this is an example of good sportsmanship or fair play. No other sport allows spectators in such close proximity to engage in possibly disruptive activity within a player's sight lines. Baseball, football, soccer or hockey fans are all physically seated a further distance away at their games. Baseball even removed white shirts and therefore customers from centerfield bleachers, so that the batter could better follow the ball. So I don't get it. Why is this allowed? Who is behind this abnormality in sports? Ah Ha! The concessionaires! I may never buy another bag of peanuts.

I ONLY HAVE TROUBLE WITH PEOPLE…

…who have no weaknesses. There's got to be something. Life would be so boring without dirty little secrets. There can be some big ones though: drug addiction…alcoholism. Medium ones too, though not necessarily less lethal: smoking… obesity. Of course, there are all sorts of sexual ones. So too, there are virtually harmless weaknesses, such as being a hoarder, a litterbug, a tattletale, a gambler. Some would say it is only human nature, because we are all sinners.

    Some of these believers strive to eradicate their weaknesses. Hiding behind their addiction to religion, they pride themselves in their moral superiority. The problem is they don't hesitate to mention that fact, over and over again. Rather than be frowned upon by these "know it alls," I prefer to hang with the imperfect. It's more interesting being with and being " a work in progress."

I ONLY HAVE TROUBLE WITH PEOPLE...

...who won't compromise. I'm not saying one shouldn't have principles or standards. I'm referring to those who absolutely refuse to consider compromise no matter what the circumstances. I do not see how one can travel through this life with such an arrogant attitude. Wouldn't life be friendless? Wouldn't such a person be lonely?

    I have a feeling such persons have a hearing problem. They can't really hear what another is saying. Therefore they cannot fully understand another's point of view. Or maybe they're just not listening or willing to listen. They just don't care. But they must have enablers...people in their lives who lack self-esteem (there's that word again) who don't question them or demand to be heard themselves. Gives me the "willies."

I ONLY HAVE TROUBLE WITH PEOPLE…

…who teach their children to be loud. I don't think people do this intentionally. It's probably something that happens for momentary convenience. If the parent is in one room and the kids are in another, instead of physically moving, the adult will yell, "DINNER'S READY!" Likewise, the kids scream back, "IN A MINUTE!"

"NOW!"

"OKAY!"

A pleasant enough exchange, but loud. When someone is listening to music or watching television, how often does anyone mute or use the pause button, when entering into a conversation? Noooo…just talk over it. Then there is the rather sad situation, when the parent is preoccupied with something or someone else and a toddler wants attention. What starts out as "Mommy, Mommy" or "Daddy, Daddy," which upon being ignored or told "Just a minute" several times, becomes an hysterical "MOMMYAHMOMMEEE" or "DADDYWHADADDEEE!" It shouldn't have to be that way, that embarrassing, that loud.

I ONLY HAVE TROUBLE WITH PEOPLE…

…who like high heels. What causes normally sane women to wear spindly spike heeled shoes? You know you're never going to make it through the entire evening. Many think they flatter their legs. That may be true, but only if you know how to walk in them. Most women could really use some lessons and hours of practice. But then you'd learn early on how extremely painful artificially elevated heels can be.

Ultimately, the lunacy of this fashion will catch up with everyone…the sore arches, the bunions, the corns, the weak ankles, varicose veins. Unlike in the show THE PRODUCERS, you won't be dancing and doing cartwheels with those walkers. Though men don't have to suffer any of the consequences, they must share the blame. Do they enjoy their females clinging on to their arms while teetering on their stilettos? Do they secretly not want women to be able to walk confidently out in front of them? Is this a sinister plot to "keep women in their place?" Isn't this like the old Chinese custom of binding women's feet?

I ONLY HAVE TROUBLE WITH PEOPLE...

...who still smoke. I have empathy for those who are addicted. As I've mentioned previously, I don't believe anyone is without weakness nor should we overly concern ourselves with trying to achieve perfection. If that were possible, it would be so boring. If, perhaps, anyone believes they have attained that level, they would be delusional. So by all means, I encourage imperfection, eccentricities, blemishes. I just wish smokers wouldn't fool themselves. Smokers may enjoy their habit for many years, but probably not long after they reach the grand old age of 50 or 60. It's hard to convince kids in their teens, young adults in their twenties and even those terribly optimistic thirty somethings, that they aren't going to live forever. In fact, I kind of like the idea of living with the attitude that you might. Makes one more adventurous. But there should be a clear demarcation between taking chances with careers or relationships and taking chances with your health. The obvious point being that a body can engage in copious opportunities and experiences, but a body can never be more than one body.

I really have no idea how to change smokers' behavior. Each individual has to make up his/her own mind. That's the only way real change can ever happen. But they're dancing to the wrong music. " I'm Sorry", the tune needs to change from "Smoke Gets in Your Eyes" to " I Can See Clearly Now."

I ONLY HAVE TROUBLE WITH PEOPLE...

...who threaten children. There are too many instances when parents have lost control and impulsively challenge their children . " If you do this...or you don't do that, I will...or will not do such and such." Without thinking, the adult has just put him/herself in a box. I don't think it takes a kid very long to figure out, " I have the upper hand." This is exactly the opposite of what the parent wishes to accomplish. What is the term? The law of unintended consequences? In order for the adult to use parental powers effectively, one must follow through on one's words. A promise is a promise and a threat is a threat. I would advise if ice cream is offered as a reward, you have a carton in the freezer. Likewise, if the child's misbehavior causes the parent to say, "I've had enough! I'm leaving!" you better be in your own home and simply exiting the room, not the house. A child being abandoned in a mall or the playground or the swimming pool is, at the very least, unacceptable behavior on your part.

Perhaps it's criminal. There is no sensible way to carry out that threat. It should never have been made. Still, it can get worse. Others can become involved. "If you don't stop that, I'm not taking you to see Grandma." Poor Granny. So if you don't agree with me, that threats are a very weak parenting technique and should be avoided if at all possible, I'm going to stop writing. (I have my fingers crossed).

I ONLY HAVE TROUBLE WITH PEOPLE…

…who try too hard to make people laugh. Anyone who has witnessed an open mike night at a comedy club will know what I mean. I'm not criticizing the venue. I think it's a great idea to offer a stage and an audience to "unknowns" to test and perfect their routines. Many, many major talents have traveled this route and achieved great success. I just think that as a "comedian" develops, he/she should be able to assess how well things are going. Probably the laughter or lack thereof would offer a clue. Yet, from my experience as an audience member, many aspiring comics are deaf. Their three to five minute sets seem like eternity. The silence is embarrassing …for the spectators. Yet, seemingly, not for the "entertainer." They go on and on. They keep coming back. How can the "artist" be so oblivious? I expect you need a healthy amount of ego just to get up on that stage. It can be very lonely up there. As a stand-up comic, you're on your own. So, who is there to help them break this habit? Not I. A long time ago, I was involved in casting the road company of a comedy out of New York. I put thumbs down on Diane Keaton.

I ONLY HAVE TROUBLE WITH PEOPLE...

...who only believe what they want to believe. Why would people be so insecure that they only listen to or read opinions that support their own philosophies? If they are so convinced of their positions, wouldn't they be able to face any opposing points of view? Wouldn't finding their ideas upheld in a challenge be a confirmation worth having? At the very least, acknowledging the opposition could provide a genuine source of amusement. If you can't stand to have your views questioned, maybe you haven't questioned them enough yourself. If your rationalization is you believe something because you believe it, maybe you haven't done your homework. How can that be satisfactory? Perhaps, if the matter is purely religious. But even then, people do find substance in their religion that is not solely faith-based. The benefits of charitable acts can be documented. Righteous deeds are often rewarded. Morally offensive actions are indeed punishable, having been incorporated into laws. I guess it just depends on how much of your life, of your reasoning, is something for which you do not want to be held responsible. The more irrationality infiltrates your rational the harder it must be to be open-minded. Don't you ever wonder what you're missing?

I ONLY HAVE TROUBLE WITH PEOPLE…

…who grow up too fast. I don't think anything can be done about "old souls." You know what I mean…those kindergartners who already act like little old men and women. And I really feel sorry for children who are forced by circumstance beyond their understanding and not of their own making to take on adult responsibilities, because the adults in their lives are incapable of doing so. But for the rest of us, I like the idea that the 80's are the new 60's, the 60's are the new 40's. However, after that feel good message, one has to be a little more reasonable and continue on that the 40's are the new 30's and the 30's are the new 20's. With improvements in modern medicine and the lessening of social pressure, there need not be a rush to marry and start a family and buy a house, etc. The new 20's can be an extension of the college years. After all, entering the real world, no longer governed by an academic structure, is in itself a true continuation of ones' "higher education."

A person could take ones' time pursuing different job opportunities, broadening ones' social circle, traveling, even living in different places. I'm not suggesting mooching off your parents. I did mention the word "job." And I'm not offering an easy way to hide from reality. I would hope the new 20's would be a time of freedom to explore and experience while reflecting on your youthful past. Hopefully, it was a youthful past. The sure way to grow up too fast is to get caught up in commercialism…buy into all the trends. Lots of make-up and skimpy clothes for pre-teen girls. Dare I say, cigarettes, tattoos and drugs for the guys? I guess I'm suggesting " Go slow" in order to " Grow old slowly."

I ONLY HAVE TROUBLE WITH PEOPLE…

…who are security risks. This subject is not as simple as it may appear. People who walk down the street talking on cell phones have diminished our personal security. Think about it. When I was growing up (slowly) if you saw someone walking down the street by him/herself, talking away, you could assume that something was wrong with that character. Your safety antennae would automatically click in. You could be crossing paths with a loony. You would be on full alert should the person do anything suspicious. You might avoid the individual, cross the street, go in the opposite direction or run. Nowadays, these persons are given cover by cell phone users. You must assume that the person walking alone, chatting away, is on a cell phone or has an 'earpiece.' If you didn't, you would be needlessly dashing across the street, running in different directions, acting like the loony.

I ONLY HAVE TROUBLE WITH PEOPLE..

…who are chauvinists. I'm sorry that I feel I must include this topic. You would have thought this term would have become an anachronism by the 21st century. But not unlike racism and homophobia, male chauvinism often lies in the hole, cards that are not revealed unless you call the bluff.

Unhappily, it seems to me, we will suffer as a country, because we will be denied a woman president. People will "talk the talk", but not "walk the walk" to the polls. How do we go about erasing the stereotypes? "A woman cannot be Commander in Chief." My God, the television show didn't even last a season. " How can a woman be trusted to make rational decisions when experiencing PMS, let alone menopause?" Too weak. Too emotional. Such illogical thinking runs rampant.

The chauvinist can't get past SEX. It can't be just coincidence that past female world leaders, Margaret Thatcher and Golda Meir come to mind, did not personify SEX. I believe Indira Gandhi was an attractive woman, but she was pretty much covered up.

America basically eliminates one-half the potential talent in the highest echelons of our political arena, because they have boobs. Then there are the traps set out for women if they should try to showcase their strength and determination. " Doesn't she sound shrill? Angry?" She probably doesn't, but this brings to mind more negative stereotypes of the nagging, possessive scold of a wife. Who wants that in your living room delivering the "State of the Union?" Why is it that "feminism" has gotten such a bad rap, while the chauvinist goes merrily on his way, basically unnoticed, but certainly not innocuous?

I ONLY HAVE TROUBLE WITH PEOPLE...

...who do not understand boobs. I believe there are two primary justifications for women's breasts. The first is to nurse the newborn. The second is to attract men, so that the first can take place. It's really that simple. I don't understand why this causes such a brouhaha, from both sexes. Horror of Horrors!
" Women should not breastfeed in public. Is there no modesty?" Never mind that more cleavage and breast is exposed and actually visible on the red carpet prior to an awards ceremony. You would really have to push your nose in there, which you can't do, because that's where the baby's nose is. Personally, I never breastfed in public. I simply preferred the alone time with my child. I could relax and I felt that somehow that would increase my infant's satisfaction. I don't think I'd like the judgmental or prying eyes. People are going to look. They may gawk. They may sneak a peek.

That's only natural, because, as I've mentioned, that's my second justification. True, there are many ways for a woman to attract a sexual partner. Personality and intelligence can be just as effective as physical traits. But, to be honest, physical assets are easier, more obvious.

Now, not all males are breast men, which is good, because, I'm sure you've noticed, not all women are created equal. Fortunately, we have men who check out legs, faces, ankles, feet, booty. I would suggest that it is not somehow wrong or immoral to play up your personal "favorables." Just don't pad your resume.

I ONLY HAVE TROUBLE WITH PEOPLE...

...who distance themselves from the ocean. I realize that some people don't get the chance to go to the ocean. I can only hope that someday, somehow, you will. As for myself, I really don't experience the ocean to the depths that so many others do. I don't snorkel or deep sea dive. I've never been on a cruise. All I can do is watch surfers in amazement. I'm really too chicken to swim with the dolphins, much less the whales. But what I most enjoy is simply walking barefoot along the shoreline. I grew up within a few blocks of Lake Michigan. As a kid I loved to go to the beach and jump the waves. But I have noticed that the big difference between jumping the waves in a lake and jumping waves in the ocean is the sand will still be there after you make that leap in the lake. In even the shallowest waters of the ocean as the water comes on shore, the sand beneath it, and you, goes out. I think this is one of Mother Nature's little jokes. It is a very difficult challenge for me to stay upright as I stroll along the beach.

I remember once seeing a man sitting at the edge of the shore, legs stretched out before him, leaning on his hands propping him up from behind, fully enjoying the sensation of the waves lapping gently over his lower body. Then the next thing I saw was this person being rolled over in a backward somersault, heels wildly wheeling over his head. However, his head was in the sand now. I think there's a life lesson to be learned from the ocean.

I ONLY HAVE TROUBLE WITH PEOPLE…

…who don't vote. I have a hard time getting my mind around the fact that one-half of the population of the United States does not vote. When our government claims to be the number one proponent of democracy in the world, the ideal model to which all should aspire, the figures do not add up. Reality does not support our rhetoric or our reputation. My personal experience with non-voters is limited, but immediate…my own son. It took several years and many, many conversations to spur him into action. It seems to me, that after years of formal education, young adults do not feel involved in society. Is this the fault of the students, the educators or the parents that the younger generation does not feel a connection ? The broader world, represented by government, is something they cannot relate to. The young adults that do… seem to have been brainwashed. It seems to be inaccurate to refer to them as young adults, because they don't seem to be capable of independent thinking, blindly following others without serious questioning and analysis. Still, there are other non-voting "adults", who cannot be "excused" for "youthful alienations".

Who of those hasn't heart the call "GET OUT THE VOTE"!? Why is this cry ignored? Are the nonexistent voters too busy? Too lazy? Too ignorant? Too complacent? Too ill? Just too pleased with how well everything is going? Too afraid they'll mess it up? Worst of all, too pessimistic…thinking our government is hopeless …not worth the effort? I don't know. But I think it would be worth our while to find out how to encourage our electorate to greater participation. I think our country, our democracy, would be better off knowing. Then maybe our reputation would rise to meet our idealized rhetoric.

I ONLY HAVE TROUBLE WITH PEOPLE…

…who do vote. If solidifying a political position on abortion or gay marriage or gun control supercedes war, world affairs, economics, education, jobs, health care, some voters "can't see the forest for the trees". I think such voters are voting their comfort level. They must think larger issues are above their pay scale. Where's that self-esteem I worry about? Where's a desire to keep informed or even to continue ones' education? Without some basic knowledge of at least some of the facts involved, they may cast their vote based on a candidate's personality. What a leap of faith!

I ONLY HAVE TROUBLE WITH PEOPLE…

…who don't like to cook. I don't get it. What's not to like? People are natural putterers and the kitchen is a perfect place in which to putter. So I'm not talking about frantically dashing to put dinner on the table after a full day's work. I'm thinking instead of taking advantage of what cooking can do for you.

Who can resist wielding a large, sharp knife? Whether you are carving a turkey or chopping an onion, you are releasing tension in a healthy manner. Likewise, the whirling of the blender, the beating of those eggs, the scraping of the carrots, the mashing of potatoes, the whipping of cream are all quite violent actions in reality. Then there are the relaxation techniques of folding an omelet, patting hamburger patties or melting butter. The creative artist can decorate cookies or birthday cakes. Adventuresome types can experiment with new recipes, perhaps inventing their own. Even the language associated with cooking can be provocative or suggestive. The bacon sizzles. The common frankfurter is a "hot" dog, a red "hot", a wiener. Yum…spicy. A pinch of this, a pinch of that.

What's more, things never get boring. Who hasn't burnt something? It could be the roast or it could be your arm.   Who hasn't bloodied themselves? There is the possibility of high drama – everyday - right in your own home. As I asked before, what's not to like?

I ONLY HAVE TROUBLE WITH PEOPLE...

... who can't admit they have lied. First of all, people should realize they do lie. If one doesn't, or if one feels incapable of lying, what a mean person she/he must be. If you can't tell a woman who has just had a catastrophic visit to the beauty shop, " It really isn't that bad" or a hostess whose dinner is slightly overdone, "It really is quite tasty", then you're not being polite. If you can't tell a beer-bellied guy, " You must have just started your exercise program" or a balding gentleman, " How dignified you look," then you're not even trying to be helpful. If you can't tell a child who failed a test, " You can do better than this" or a kid who lost a game, "You'll get 'em next time," then you're lacking a humanitarian gene. Whether these little white lies are meant to be tactful, comforting or optimistic, you are alleviating an unpleasant situation and not hurting anyone. That should count for something. On the other hand, if you have really told a whopper and there are those who never blink an eye when doing so, it is often the case that not apologizing for it is worse than the lie itself. Sadly, I don't think I have to expound on this last statement. Our politicians have offered many excellent examples of such as of late.

I ONLY HAVE TROUBLE WITH PEOPLE...

...who just drop by. What are telephones for? I guess these folks, who just "happen to be in the neighborhood," don't know. I thought the day of just stopping by without a warning was relegated to quaint remembrances of the past - something people did in the fifties. Well, I didn't care for the practice in the fifties either. The unexpected visitor may think I have nothing to do. That may be true, but it is my prerogative to do nothing. Do you think I want you to know that? Privacy is first and foremost. It should be protected over all else. Of course, one must make allowances for persons whose jobs depend on interrupting ones' privacy. The Fed Ex man, the florist delivery boy, the mail lady who needs a signature, they all want to find you at home and since they often are bringing lovely surprises, deserve amnesty. Otherwise, give me a call, so I can put you off, or leave a note, after I don't answer the door. I really hate hiding behind the curtains until you go away.

I ONLY HAVE TROUBLE WITH PEOPLE…

…who don't give credit when credit is due. I sympathize with those Oscar and Emmy winners who aren't allowed to thank the hundreds of people responsible for the award they are receiving. I sincerely believe, given the opportunity, they would list every single person they had met along the path to their success. After all, they like being in front of a camera. Face time is where it's at. But even if their motives are not all that admirable, the desire to thank people is.

There is no excuse for plagiarists who, whether through naivety, laziness, sloppiness or underhandedness, neglect to acknowledge their sources. Not too long ago, I was pleased to see some amateur film footage, taken by my late father, on a PBS interview program. My 90 year old mother and I were eager to see the credits role. To see a loved ones' name on the tube would be a special thrill for us. But it wasn't there. I assumed this was merely an oversight. I contacted the station and explained my situation. There must have been some effort by the programmers to check out my story and examine their sources, because when the show was rerun, an additional credit appeared. Thank you PBS.

I ONLY HAVE TROUBLE WITH PEOPLE...

...who can grow things. Since I have recently moved to Southern California, I've become increasingly aware of plants, flowers, foliage. Always something is in bloom or blooming or about to bloom, except, of course, in my plot and pots. It seems that most trees and bushes follow their own natural cycles. I can enjoy that. What I don't understand is why people have this conceit that they can improve on sumptuous surroundings. But they do. They tend to gorgeous gardens, spectacular window boxes, even awe-inspiring flower pots. They grow things. I guess that's why I have trouble with them, because I can't. And I'm jealous. Jealousy is not a good feeling to have. So what does one do to get over this disabilitating trait? Face it head on. I tried to understand their passion. I tried to plant seeds, only to see them dug up by birds and squirrels, even cats. I repotted plants. I added soil. In desperation I laid down a pre-seeded roll of wildflowers. I watered and waited. Nothing.

Then, about five years ago, my mother received a potted orchid for her birthday. My mother was in a nursing home at the time, so after the flower faded, I took it to my home and, following instructions, I cut it back. The next year the orchid came back. I repeated the operation and it came back the next year, the next year and the next. Aren't orchids supposed to be very delicate and difficult to handle? I was so proud. Then, sadly, my mother died and the orchid didn't come back.

I ONLY HAVE TROUBLE WITH PEOPLE…

…who bring stuff. I don't want to sound ungrateful, but why do people bring food or drink to a get-together where it is a known fact food and drink will be provided? Isn't it an underhanded insult to the host or hostess? Aren't they insinuating that the party givers have forgotten something? That they know better what the guests would enjoy? If they can't resist this impulse, they should attend potluck dinners only. Or better yet, why don't they throw their own party? I would be happy to attend and not bring anything.

I ONLY HAVE TROUBLE WITH PEOPLE…

…who have not vacationed at a dude ranch. I grew up watching Hopalong Cassidy, Roy Rogers, Gene Autrey and The Cisco "Hey Pancho" Kid on TV. I was put on a horse at the ripe old age of two and have been crazy about horses ever since. While growing up, my absolutely favorite family vacations were at dude ranches in Colorado and Montana. Therefore, my own family was destined to eleven years of family vacations at a little ranch in Wisconsin.

Americans have always prided themselves in their "pioneering spirit." We are fascinated by stories of the "Old West." We have idolized the "cowboy image" from Will Rogers to John Wayne to Ronald Reagan. I believe everyone should experience a little taste of our country's history. I'm not suggesting reliving a realistic frontier lifestyle, such as that depicted on such PBS mini series as TEXAS RANCH HOUSE (1850 something).

A dude ranch is for "dudes." Even at the most basic, there'll be a swimming pool, probably shuffleboard. You won't be eating around an open campfire or sleeping in a sleeping bag (unless you sign up for it). There are many wonderful memories to be made on any family vacation, but there's something about the smell of horse manure, I promise you, your family will never ever forget.

I ONLY HAVE TROUBLE WITH PEOPLE…

…who don't respect their limitations. This can cause serious complications. There are those who suffer from bulimia or anorexia. What ever happened to simply counting calories? What about the average swimmer who goes out a little too far in the ocean? How about the neophyte lone hiker blazing a new trail? These possible tragedies seemingly endanger only the one person. However, when the person is in a position of power, the consequences are greatly magnified. CEOs have recently been exposed for their unchecked arrogance and greed, the results being catastrophic for employees, pensioners and shareholders. There are ongoing investigations of corruption at all levels of government for which the trusting taxpayers pay the price. Dare I say, there are politicians who do not recognize they may have intellectual limitations? No one person can be expected to have expertise in all areas that confront today's world, but policy makers are in the unique position of being able to draw upon the finest of minds. Do recent events suggest that they do not do so?

I ONLY HAVE TROUBLE WITH PEOPLE...

...who make you wonder why you want to eat out. It seems that more and more restaurants, I assume to provide the most possible seating, set tables for two or four rather close together. While this may facilitate the flow of customers, it also makes eavesdropping almost mandatory. The difficulty arises when the subject matter is not conducive to a pleasant dining experience. People either must have forgotten that their conversation is taking place in public or think that their stories are worthy of an audience. I beg to differ. I do not wish to hear details of root canals or colonoscopies with my osso bucco.

I have actually witnessed a family reunion at Denny's. I don't object to their motivation, just the location - immediately just inside the doors of the crowded eatery. People, unfamiliar with the "family," are waiting for tables, trying to place their names on the waiting list, paying their bills, trying to leave, while the "family" is greeting arriving members with all sorts of hugging and kissing. Screaming introductions of "Little Susie, you must remember Great Auntie So and So." "Little Susie! I can't believe how you've grown!" <u>I can't</u> believe you all are blocking the entrance, causing a logjam and irritating so many innocent strangers.

There is also the case of the overly conscientious restaurant employee, whose shift is probably just about over. In the midst of your dinner, he/she starts to vacuum the rugs or sweep the floors, eventually intruding on your space. There is no excuse for this, unless your coordinately challenged waiter has tragically dumped serving trays of food on or around your lap. As for such a hapless waiter, that's a throw back to respecting your limitations.

I ONLY HAVE TROUBLE WITH PEOPLE…

…who try to make everything equal. It's a nice idea. After all, our founders wrote in the Declaration of Independence " all men are created equal." The only catch is if you attempt to apply that principle you only create more problems. Ever try to serve perfectly equal sized portions of ice cream to a couple of four year olds? You'll have the same difficulty with slices of birthday cake. Don't even try to explain to siblings that you love them all equally. Well meaning lawmakers promoted Affirmative Action only to be attacked from the right, left and center. " Are you implying that those of African descent need special assistance?" " Should there be preferential treatment that limits the opportunities for those more qualified?" "We have come such a long way Affirmative Action is no longer needed." Then there's Title IX. What's wrong with offering women the same advantages in collegiate sports as men? Plenty, I guess, according to the ruckus it caused. "The entire men's rowing and wrestling teams have been eliminated to make room for one female golfer!" My, my.

Maybe the writers of the Declaration of Independence weren't really serious. The document doesn't claim that men and women are created equal or that slavery thereby should no longer exist. Maybe they realized that applying that principle would indeed create more problems, so they simply ignored any follow-through. But, to our credit, later-day Americans did not. Progress on the issue of equality, though always a sticky-wicket, has been confronted from time to time, though not always for causes that deserve the banner of equality. I would suggest the idea of the theory of intelligent design being taught along with the theory of evolution in science classes to be an excessive desire to make everything equal.

   Do we give up on the promise of equality because it presents so many difficulties? Equality in education…in health care…in financial opportunities. I think our governmental officials could do the writers of the Declaration one better by realizing that we are not truly created equal if we do not have equal access to a social structure which honors the " unalienable rights of Life, Liberty and the pursuit of Happiness." So, if I may, I'd like to revise this musing. There are some things, though not EVERYTHING, worth the trouble.

I ONLY HAVE TROUBLE WITH PEOPLE…

…who never had long hair. I have had a ponytail since sixth grade. There have been times in my life when I questioned my lengthy decision. When I entered college (needed a clear break from high school), when I turned 21 (beginning of adulthood), then 25 (a quarter of a century) then 30 (now a mother) 40 (when, as they say, "life begins?") 50 (when middle age begins) then 60 (when people start calling you "ma'am") I "kept on keeping on" my ponytail. Of course, I realize men are limited in the hair growing department. Often to their dismay in their later years. Yet I would congratulate hippies for their hairdos. I support mothers whose male toddlers sport Prince Valiant pageboys. You may experience some discomfort when your little Michael is mistaken for a little girl, but you are allowing him a sensation he most likely will not ever have again in his entire life. That feeling of hair tickling the back of his neck. Maybe, dare I say, even swishing further down his back? Men grow all kinds of beards and sideburns and mustaches and goatees, but, I believe, that's all to make up for not being able to know the tingly, titillating touch of having long hair. Face it, there's a little bit of CHER in all of us.

I ONLY HAVE TROUBLE WITH PEOPLE…

…who do not pick up after themselves. Why is it that some people feel it necessary to leave a trail? Are they all seriously obsessed with Hansel and Gretel? They came away from that fairy tale with the belief the lesson to be learned was "It was all the kids' fault. They brought it upon themselves. That was stupid to drop bread crumbs along the way. Always leave something more permanent." Let everybody know you have passed this way. You exist. The proof of your existence is the mess you have left behind. Kids tend to leave toys where last they played with them. Every parent who has stepped barefooted on a Tonka truck realizes that this carelessness is not painless. The problem of litterbugs is a national disgrace. Are we just spoiled? Always expecting someone else to do our dirty work? Sometimes I get the impression that this is the most common cause of nagging. There should be a study about how many divorces this issue has caused. We could call it "The Brothers Grimm" grounds for divorce.

I ONLY HAVE TROUBLE WITH PEOPLE...

...who shower every single day of their lives. I'm not referring to people who do dirty work. And I mean, literally, dirty work. There would be thousands of health reasons to turn on that faucet. But there are so many millions who hardly break a sweat during the day. Of course, there are those exercise over-achievers, who will need to lather up. But from viewing the general public everyday, they are a minority. As for the rest of us, we are dehydrating our skin. We who are obsessed with premature aging are just asking for wrinkled, dry, flaky flesh. Oh, but after that daily dousing, you can always pile on the moisturizing creams, which in turn immediately plug up your pores, negating any positive effect of the cleansing. I think we should realize we have been brainwashed. We have been sold a bill of goods. As well as lots and lots of soap and body wash. We are not that filthy of a bunch.

I ONLY HAVE TROUBLE WITH PEOPLE…

…who take up too much space. I simply don't understand why people need to live in mansions. Do people really need dozens of bedrooms and bathrooms? It must be a very complicated life. Think of how many decisions you would have to make over the simplest things. I would imagine you would have to have intercom systems or how could you keep track of the members of the household? Unless that's the point. You could care less where they would be. I can't help thinking of families with small children squeezed into a one-room apartment, sleeping more than two to a bed. The disproportionate space occupied by the high and mighty and the less fortunate symbolizes the disparity of wealth in this country. It highlights what has become the inequality of the American dream.

Those who are grossly overweight certainly take up too much space. At one time, heft was a sign of prosperity, but nowadays most would prefer to shed a few pounds. Perhaps, those who take up too much space in their lifestyle will one day realize it would be better for all if they let go of some things. Not necessarily in pounds, but in privileges.

I ONLY HAVE TROUBLE WITH PEOPLE…

…who tell me things I just don't want to know.
I am just amazed at the personal things that people, you hardly know, will tell you. And you haven't asked. You hadn't encouraged them. You've not even been particularly polite or inviting. Most often, the subject seems to be their physical problems. Or intimate details of the physical problems of their relatives or friends… people you were not even aware existed until you learned of their traumas. They must suffer from an overwhelming desire to "share." And their sounding board must suffer too, because I can't think of a courteous way to wiggle out of the situation. You may try to avoid the person in the future, but then you're living with the irrational fear that someday, somewhere, waiting round the bend…WHAMO! But then again, looking on the bright side, they gave me this paragraph for my book.

I ONLY HAVE TROUBLE WITH PEOPLE…

…who never change their mind. I don't have an affinity for people who are fickle and certainly not for people who are unstable. I think it would be wonderful if everyone gave considerable and careful deliberation to their ideas before adopting them. But they don't. So I don't think it is unreasonable during ones' lifetime, as one gains experience and advances their education, to admit that they had been wrong and change their mind. Yet, there are folks who find that impossible. I'd like to know how one could be so immoveable. Is it pride? Ego? Hubris? Stubbornness? These are not very admirable character traits. The term "flip flopping" has been more or less bludgeoned to death in recent years. I suggest we do the same for "pigheadedness."

I ONLY HAVE TROUBLE WITH PEOPLE…

…who don't have trouble with people. I really believe that there is a problem with people who are too, too happy…too, too pleased with themselves. They give the " Pollyannas" of the world a bad name. They may very well be exceptionally satisfied with their own lives, but they can't be paying attention. They must be oblivious of others who are not as fortunate. They must lack the ability to empathize. If they don't see or feel there are problems, they can't possibly be called upon to help remedy them. They are truly ignorant. I'm afraid there seem to be more and more members of our society who refuse to face reality, who don't let the facts intrude upon their world view, who are immune to the truth. How sad.

I ONLY HAVE TROUBLE WITH PEOPLE...

...who can't step back. We've all seen those cartoons where Wile E. Coyote is running so fast, he has lost control of his gangly limbs and can't stop himself. He suddenly realizes his tragic fate as he plunges over the edge of a cliff. We are amused. But in real life, we can put events into place that take on a life of their own. We may find ourselves no longer in control. It's no longer amusing.

No matter how driven or committed a person may be or how significant or challenging the task, I believe a certain amount of perspective could be gained by stepping back once in a while. You may need to hear the opinions of others. You may still be able to put the brakes on or slow down the pace of "unintended consequences." You may be able to change course entirely.

Then again, you may only need to retune the ukulele. You may simply find a break relaxing. Maybe things aren't so bad after all. You reenter the ring refreshed. Ready for Round II. Pardon me, while I step back.

www.ingramcontent.com/pod-product-compliance
Lightning Source LLC
LaVergne TN
LVHW051838080426
835512LV00018B/2955